barcelona
gastronomy and cuisine

Photography Oriol Aleu
Cuisine and stylism Ana Torróntegui
Texts Toni Monné
Graphic design Joseta Torróntegui

TRIANGLE ▼ POSTALS

barcelona_cuisine

© Triangle Postals S.L.
Pere Tudurí, 8 · 07710 Sant Lluís, Menorca
www.triangle.cat

Coordination and publication of the project: Oriol Aleu
Cuisine, stylism: Ana Torróntegui
Adaptation and revision of the recipes: Toni Monné
Texts: Toni Monné
Graphic design and layout: Joseta Torróntegui
Photographic production assistant: Oriol Roset
Photography: Oriol Aleu
Translation: Steve Cedar
First edition in English: 2011

P.: 9, 12, 15, 33, 35 © photos: Arxiu fotogràfic de Barcelona
P.: 8, 10 © Biblioteca de Catalunya
P.: 15 © Fundació Josep Pla, col. M. Lluïsa Massort
P.: 22, 23, 24 © photos: Fototeca, El Bulli
P.: 18 © Ateneu Barcelonès
P.: 32 © Arxiu Històric de la Ciutat de Barcelona (AHCB)

ISBN: 978-84-8478-498-2
Registration no.: B-19.877 - 2011

Printed by: Sanvergrafic 7-2013
Printed in Barcelona

Gaudí, and many other Modernist architects, used attractive mosaics on their buildings made with broken pieces of ceramic joined with mortar. They were fragments of tiles, tea cups or enamelled plates, in bright colours and of diverse origins that, together with a new composition that had nothing in common with their original designs, managed to create a marvellous aesthetic effect. This technique was known by the Catalan word of *trencadís*, the etymology of which we find in the verb *trencar*, which means "break" or "fragment".

The cuisine of Barcelona is a type of grand *trencadís* formed over the centuries by very diverse influences.

In this book we have tried to explain, in a very general and informative way, this open, multiple and cosmopolitan character of the city's gastronomy. We have wanted to suggest a brief and engaging stroll around some products, some recipes and a few emblematic spots.

They are only fragments of a large puzzle that could be put together in very diverse ways and in which inevitably different pieces appear day by day. This is because what today may seem new, exotic and avant-garde to us, will perhaps be completely integrated in the city's classical cuisine tomorrow.

Introduction 05

The cuisine of the Barcelona people 08

From the traditional inn to the vanguard 16

The aperitif and tapas 27

The city of cafés 32

The world of sweets 38

The capital of chocolate 42

La Boqueria: the cathedral of the senses 48

The markets in the city 58

Barceloneta: the city in the sea 63

Peas from Llavaneres 74

D.O. Alella wines 78

Cherries from Baix Llobregat 82

Artichokes from El Prat 86

Blue-footed chicken from El Prat 90

D.O. Cava 94

Places with flavour 102

Recipes 136

The cuisine of the Barcelona people

If you ask any citizen of Barcelona about the typical cuisine of their city, they will probably reply that they do not have a very clear and concise answer. They will almost certainly mention the existence of some recipes such as cod *a la llauna*, the *botifarra* sausage or pork with kidney beans, cannelloni or the now almost forgotten fish and seafood casserole.

It will also be difficult for the citizen in question to explain the relationship that these dishes have with the cuisine of the city. It would be an even more arduous task to find someone who provides us with a minimally coherent explanation of the historic development of Barcelona's cuisine.

Due to its strategic location as an important goods port with trade relations throughout the Mediterranean, flanked by two rivers, the Llobregat and the Besòs, which, descending from the Pyrenees, ensured waterways with the inland towns, Barcelona has always had a cosmopolitan and open character, both seafaring and mountain in nature, from which it became the *Ciutat Comtal*, the city of the counts, and brought together the small feudal states that were created due to the Frankish weakness after fighting the Muslims.

The first news of the gastronomic sphere that appears documented about the territory date back to the Greek geographer Strabo, who praised the quality of the oysters of Tarraco and Barcino. And, in the time of the Romans, they extolled the excellence of *garum* or *múria*, a popular sauce that was made from fermenting blue fish in brine, above all mackerel, and which was exported to other parts of the Empire.

Catalan medieval cuisine was one of the most solid and prestigious in the entire Middle Ages. The recipe book of Rupert de Nola is an example of refined, tasty and aristocratic cuisine, highly reputed and influential in its time.

In the Middle Ages the city became the regular centre of the itinerant court of the counts of Barcelona and the monarchs of Aragon. The cuisine of Gothic Barcelona was characterised by a sophistication that would require a large number of spices and condiments.

To the left in the centre, 1520 edition of the *Llibre del Coch*, conserved in the Biblioteca de Catalunya.

Above, historical photo of a street market in La Rambla.

In the 15th and 16th centuries Barcelona was a city in a process of population growth, which obliged the authorities to control the conditions of food sales. The *Consell de Cent* (Council of One Hundred) had a municipal post specially designated to control the markets and keep an eye out for frauds: the *Mostassaf*.

The urban orchards already showed in this period that they were unable to supply the needs of a growing population. Thus the concept of *l'hort i el vinyet* (the orchard and the vineyard) was developed in all the towns and territories that surrounded the city. Broad beans and young garlic were cultivated in April; peas in May; pumpkins, from June to September, which formed part of one of the most

Spectacular example of Modernist style in the Escribà confectioner's in La Rambla.

popular dishes of the time, seasoned with cinnamon and almond milk; Swiss chard, aubergines, cucumbers, spinach and onions. Vegetables would often be combined with pulses such as lentils, kidney beans, chickpeas or cereals such as barley. Lots of fruit was also eaten: cherries, figs, apricots, plums, pears, grapes, peaches, melons... In winter dried fruits and nuts were popular: almonds, hazelnuts, chestnuts, figs and raisins...

The fruit and vegetables that arrived from America –tomato, pepper, potato... would change the recipe book of all the continent's cuisines forever.

Later on, the cocoa, coffee and rum trades from the overseas colonies would also leave a deep imprint on the local gastronomy.

Of special importance is the relationship with Cuba during the 19th century. The first Cuban cookbook –and also the first Catalan cookbook written in Spanish: *Nuevo Manual de la cocinera catalana y cubana* (now manual of Catalan and Cuban cuisine)– was published in 1858 by an *Americano* –which is what they called the Catalans who went to Cuba–, Joan Cabrisas, who had been a chef in the Fonda de los Tres Reyes.

On many occasions the erudite Néstor Luján defined Catalan cuisine as the result of an individual personality and an accumulation of influences closely linked to the geography. Over the base of a rural and peasant cuisine that combined the use of lard and olive oil as fats, Luján pointed out the influences

Detail of Plaça Reial, with the fountain of the Three Graces in the centre and the lampposts designed by Antoni Gaudí.

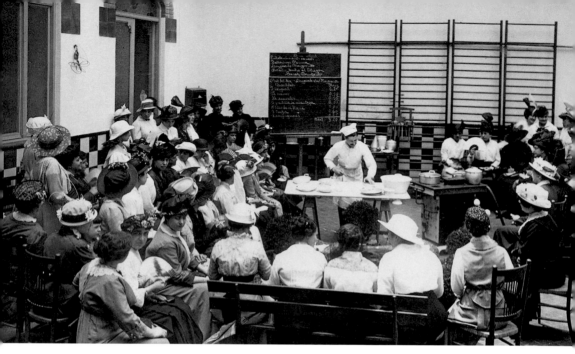

from Provence in the frequent use of herbs –thyme, rosemary, savory, marjoram, mint, oregano…–; the influence of the Baroque excesses of Valencian cuisine and the importance of the products that entered there in the Middle Ages –sugar cane, rice, oranges…–; and the impact of the strong dishes of Aragonese cuisine. *"Barcelona is the mixture of all these cuisines, since the city of counts is a capital that brings together the natural produce of all the regions of Catalonia and even the rest of Spain".*

According to Luján, aristocratic cuisine disappeared in the 18th century –illustrated perfectly in the engagement book *Calaix de Sastre* by Rafael Amat i de Cortada, Baron of Maldà–, and popular and bourgeois Catalan cuisine would continue being built over the four basic pillars: *samfaina* (a type of ratatouille), *picada* (chopped garlic, almonds and parsley), *allioli* (garlic and olive oil mayonnaise) and an onion, tomato and garlic sauce base, the *sofregits*.

Master class of cooking at the turn of the century in the Institut de la Dona Francesca Bonnemaison (AFB).

The multiple and polyhedric nature of Catalan cuisine is inherent in any regional cuisine with several centuries of history behind it. However, Barcelona has assimilated in particular –and continues assimilating– the influences of all the cuisines with which it has related throughout its history. This is undoubtedly one of its distinguishing marks.

In the mid-18th century, Italian chefs left a clear mark on opening the first restaurants (*becos*) and cafés to be known in the city. Later on would come the period of refinement of grand classical French cuisine in the more prestigious establishments of the late 19th century.

As well as medieval recipe books –*Sent Soví*, an anonymous work written in the first half of the 15th century and *El llibre del Coch* by Rupert de Nola, written before 1490– we should point out here a series of works that, later, would be very important in the spreading of Catalan cuisine among housewives. We should thus mention *La cuynera catalana*, published in instalments from 1830. In 1923, Ferran Agulló, journalist and politician, published a decisive work, *El Llibre de la cuina catalana*. The Manresa chef Ignasi Domènech, who would travel to Paris and later London in

Above, detail of the Boqueria market. Below, façade of the Colmado Quílez on the corner of Rambla Catalunya and Aragó streets.

order to consolidate his formation alongside the maestro Escoffier, published many cookbooks, some of them very popular, throughout his life. Perhaps the most influential and republished of all his books was *La teca* (1924).

Neither should we forget the impact that the classes given by the Swiss chef Josep Rondissoni in the *Institut de Cultura per la Dona* from the nineteen-twenties had on a whole generation of housewives from Barcelona's upper middle class. His cookbook *Culinaria*, published in 1945, was used to popularise some of the great classics of international, French and Catalan cuisine.

It would be unthinkable not to quote here Josep Pla, prolific author who wrote, on commission, a pioneering book about cooking and the eating habits of the Catalans. In *El que hem menjat* (1972), Pla praised traditional cuisine railing against the trivialisation that the new times brought. A few years later, in 1977, Manuel Vázquez Montalbán refuted many of his arguments in *L'art del menjar a Catalunya*.

While some speak of loss of identity due to globalisation, lack of time, the invasion of pre-cooked meals and fast food, others confirm that we are experiencing a new Golden Era thanks to

Historical photo of the arrival of the fish at the wharves of the port in Barceloneta.

the great informative work done by the media, the integration of new cultures and the popularity of chefs such as Carme Ruscalleda, Santi Santamaria, Joan Roca, Carles Gaig or Ferran Adrià –to mention a few– who have made Catalan high cuisine a worldwide benchmark.

Above, in the centre: the writer Josep Pla, one of the great promoters of Catalan gastronomy.

From the traditional inn to the vanguard

Boarding houses, inns, *becos* and restaurants

The book *El hostal, la fonda, la taberna y el café en la vida barcelonesa* (1945) by the writer Clovis Eymeric –pseudonym of Luis Almerich– constitutes one of the first serious attempts to establish a documented chronicle of the history of the Barcelona hotel and restaurant industry. Eymeric highlighted the lack of hotel tradition that existed in the city until the 18th century. *"The lords went from castle to castle; the poor, from church to church"*. The few boarding houses that existed were reserved for the *traginers* (muleteers) or travelling traders and they were in strategic points on the routes of fairs and markets.

Nevertheless, as far back as in 1393 there is news in Barcelona of the existence of a Hotel Owners Guild (*Gremi d'Hostalers*). It is documented that Pere IV had stayed several times in the *Hostal de la Bella Dona*, on the outskirts of the city. Eymeric recounts that in the 15th century there was a famous establishment known as the *Hostal de la Flor del Lliri* (Inn of the Lily Flower), close to the convent of Santa Caterina, where wealthy people and nobles used to stay in a palatial and luxurious setting that led to more than one popular legend, some of them really salacious.

Other boarding houses from the 15th century were the Hostal de Santa Eulàlia, Hostal del Lleó, Hostal del Cavall, Hostal de la Maça, Hostal de la Campana, Hostal del Senyor Infant and Hostal dels Correus, as the always extremely well-documented erudite Néstor Luján shows us in his book *Veinte siglos de cocina en Barcelona*.

The taverns, which did not have rooms for lodging, were recognisable by the branch of the green pine that was used as a door frame. This symbol later remained associated with the arrival of the *vi novell* (new wine of the year). The establishments hung a branch of green pine to inform their clients that they were now serving wine from the most recent harvest.

Kitchen of the Los Caracoles restaurant, one of the most emblematic historical restaurants of the city.

The first premises to receive the name of *fonda*, boarding house, was the Fonda de Santa Maria. It is said that the term *fonda* began here because it was reached by going down some stairs (*fonda* means "deep" or "down" in Catalan). Another etymological theory relates the word with the Arab *fondaq*, hostel or store. Later on the Hostal del Sol and. above all, the Fonda del Falcó would become popular. In the latter premises, a waiter named Batista became famous serving dishes such as pork with kidney beans, *botifarra* sausage with wild mushrooms or cod *a la llauna*. Batista wore a tailcoat the colour of a "fly's wings" and a velvet cap with a charming tassel. They say that this popular character's funeral led to mass demonstration of public mourning.

In the boarding housing *de sisos* (of sixes) one ate really well for six quarters (each quarter was three cents of a peseta). They were cheap taverns serving simple fare and without pretensions. On the menu they would inevitably serve *escudella* (thick soup) or *cap i pota* (head and leg of pork). Later, the name of *fonda de sisos* was used in a pejorative way to define restaurants with pretensions that were not up to the grade.

Before implementing the a la carte service, the boarding houses used the system called "round table". The guests came at the sound of a bell –lunch was at one and supper at eight– and sat down like a family, all together around a large table presided over by the owner of the establishment.

Above left, portrait of the charming Batista, the popular waiter of the Fonda del Falcó (Arxiu de l'Ateneu Barcelonès).

Can Culleretes opened in 1776 as a chocolate shop.
It was later transformed into a restaurant

In these boarding houses, in which meals were also served, they were also known as *becos*.

However, in general, the people of Barcelona were never that keen on eating out and the large restaurants did not become popular until the mid-19th century. The first prestigious restaurants were opened in this period, the majority of their owners being Italian or French. The cosmopolitan character of these pioneering restaurants has remained instilled in Barcelona cuisine as one of its main characteristics. Traditionally many chefs decided to extend their training in French restaurants. This is what the famous Ignasi Domènech did, who went to Paris and ended up working with the maestro Auguste Escoffier in London's luxurious Savoy Hotel.

Today, the oldest restaurant in the city still working in Can Culleretes, in Carrer Quintana. This historic establishment opened in 1786 although in the early period it operated as a *granja*, a cafeteria, or chocolate shop. They say that here you could

The age of splendour of the grand restaurants would come with the mythical Pince, Glacier, Suizo, Justin, Continental, Lion d'Or, Chez Martin, Casa Llibre or the Maison Dorée. Today all of them have disappeared. They were decades of bourgeois splendour during which the expression *el sopar de duro* (the 5 peseta-supper) was established, a banquet well worth its high price.

The Civil War and the post-war years that followed represented a serious setback for the luxury restaurants. Many of the most renowned establishments of the city were forced to close but, in the following decades, new prestigious restaurants opened and some others were reorganised. It would be impossible to mention all of them here: the Parrilla del Ritz, the Hotel Colón, Quo Vadis, Milán, Casa Leopoldo, Finisterre, Orotava, Reno, Via Véneto... Los Caracoles, the hundred-year-old establishment in Carrer Escudellers, and Can Solé, in the Barceloneta district, became must-to-be-visited restaurants by all the celebreties and luxury tourists who visited the city.

In many restaurants and hotels they imposed the so-called "international cuisine", impersonal and globalised. The lack of hotel and catering schools was an obstacle difficult to

always hear the voice of the owner ordering more clean spoons for the dining room: "*Noies, culleretes!*" (More spoons, girls!).

Also still very popular is Les 7 Portes, opened in 1840 as a cafeteria and later converted into a restaurant.

Another historic establishment that we should mention is Els 4 Gats which in its early stage (1897-1904) became the meeting place for the most representative painters of Catalan Modernism. Here is where Rusiñol, Casas, Utrillo and the young Nonell and Picasso, among many others, would meet.

overcome for several generations. At the beginning of the seventies, Ramón Cabau spread the ideas of Nouvelle Cuisine in Barcelona from his L'Agut d'Avinyò restaurant, as would Josep Mercader also do from the Motel Empordà, in Figueres.

Years later, a distinguished group of new chefs began to stand out with personal inter pretations of traditional cuisine. Modernity arrived in the early eighties with restaurants such as Vinya Rosa, Montse Guillén, Jaume de Provença, Farin, Azulete, El Vell Sarrià... many now disappeared. They, and many other creative chefs who cannot be named here for questions of space, brought to Barcelona what is today known as signature cuisine.

In the interior decoration of Els 4 Gats one can still take in the atmosphere of the Modernist period.

Vanguard stoves

The city of Barcelona will go down in the history of high cuisine thanks to a universally-known chef. Ferran Adrià, born in L'Hospitalet de Llobregat (Barcelona) in 1962, has led a gastronomic revolution that has acquired worldwide character. From his El Bulli restaurant in Roses, in the north of the Costa Brava, this revolutionary creator has shaken the foundations of high cuisine with his innovative creative approaches.

Adrià recognises that the trigger that led him to reconsider his way of understanding creativity was the maxim of the French chef Jacques Maximin: "Creating is not copying". From this, the history of

Above, the *Molls* Gaudí (red mullets). On the right, Albert Adrià, Ferran's brother and director of the Taller (workshop) with Oriol Castro.

Adrià and El Bulli has been written through dishes, recipes and techniques that have amazed chefs from all over the world.

Ferran Adrià's first book of recipes, *El Bulli: el sabor del Mediterráneo* (1993), illustrated a very revealing dish on its cover: the *Molls* Gaudí (red mullet). It consists of some fillets of red mullets deboned and covered with a mosaic of finely cut *brunoise* vegetables that recall the famous ceramic *trencadis* that adorned the creations of Gaudí. It was a declaration of principles: Adrià's creativity could find its inspiration anywhere. There were no limits.

Initially questioned, the chef amazed the world with new techniques and concepts such as the famous foams, deconstructions or spherifications. In 2000 he set up the Taller de El Bulli, a spaced devoted entirely to research, a veritable culinary laboratory of R+D, located in a small 18th-century palace in Carrer Portaferrissa, very close to the Boqueria market.

Spanish chefs recognise Adrià as the true driving force of a revolution that had its epicentre in Spain and which began to spread through specialised congresses. The creative maelstrom of these chefs received international recognition

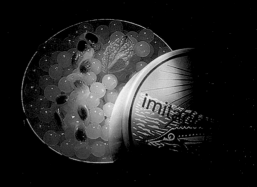

in 2003, when *The New York Times* Sunday supplement dedicated its cover to the "New Nouvelle Cuisine". Ferran Adrià appeared on the cover presenting an ethereal air of carrot. From here on, the culinary vanguard would become international.

It would be impossible to mention the group of Catalan chefs who have given a boost to this important movement. Carme Ruscalleda from Sant Pol, Carles Gaig from Barcelona or Joan Roca from Girona would perhaps be the most visible figures amongst many others.

Many young chefs have recently shown a commitment to vanguard approaches from less luxurious restaurants, in which they can feel freer and more comfortable to create and offer more accessible prices for the diner. They are known as "bistronomy", a new term that mixes the words "bistro" and "gastronomy".

Despite being a mould-breaking movement, Spanish vanguard cuisine has always shown great respect for the tradition and quality of close and local products. Moreover, the association of chefs and scientists favourable to joint research has helped in the spreading of good eating habits and has meant a giant step forward in the understanding of the physical-chemical causes entailed in any culinary process. Precisely in order to promote these advances to promote their diffusion the Alicia Foundation (*Alimentación* and *Ciencia,* food and science) has been created, situated in the spectacular monastery of Sant Benet del Bages, in the county of Bages, close to Manresa.

Above, Ferran Adrià and Oriol Castro in the full creative process. On the right, caviar of melon. Below, cabinet display of ingredients inside the Taller.

Above, Rafael Penya, chef of the restaurant Gresca.

The aperitif and *tapas*

"The custom of going for the aperitif is as old as hunger". So goes a saying as popular as it is untrue. *"Anar a fer el vermut"* (having an aperitif) assumes the ritual of sitting down at a pleasant terrace or at the bar of a crowded bar and order some tapas, generally not very enlightened (olives, cockles, anchovies, crisps or fried potatoes...) with a glass of vermouth, a small beer or soft drink to whet the appetite before a meal.

Absinthe *(Artemisia absinthum)* is an aromatic plant with a very bitter flavour. The legend goes that it gets its name from the goddess Artemis in recognition of its many medicinal properties. Hippocrates considered it a drug with therapeutic effects. In France it is known as *absinthe*; in Italy, *assenzio*; in English *wormwood*; and in German, *wermut*.

Wormwood opens up the appetite, combats digestive lethargy and dyspepsia, and is diuretic, febrifugal, vermifrugal and antiseptic. Wine with wormwood was drunk in Rome (*Vinus absintathus*) and was also known in Gaul.

Vermouth, with or without soda, is a tradition in many bars in the city.

The beer brewers of Bavaria used the word *wermoth* to name a spirit made with liquor and extract of wormwood. The mixture of wormwood and wine, which was popularised in France and Hungary, led to a thriving industry in Turin during the 18th century. The magic of this new drink lay in the in the innumerable quantity of infusions of diverse essences that were added to clarified white wine: sage, savory, coriander, lemon and bitter orange peel, camomile, vanilla, violets, roses, gentian, cinnamon, tea, sandal, quinine…

The great promoter of the goodness of vermouth in Barcelona was an Italian. Flaminio Mezzalama, representative of a large vermouth company in Turin, opened two establishments in the city in 1902: the spectacular Café Torino and a second smaller place, the Grill Room, in Carrer Escudellers which, turned into a restaurant, can still be visited today. Of course, in both premises, vermouth was the most asked-for aperitif.

Absinthe, another derivate of wormwood mixed with alcohol, possibly of Swiss origin, was

Diverse aperitifs, vermouths, absinthes... On the right, Quim Pérez in "Quimet & Quimet".

also popularised amongst the literary and artistic bohemian scene of the late 19th century.

We also highlight in this chaptor the historic importance of Moritz beer, produced in Barcelona by Louis Moritz from Alsace in the mid-19th century.

Although production halted in 1978, in 2004 the fifth and sixth generations of the family decided with great success to re-launch the legendary Barcelona beer, recovering as the headquarters the emblematic premises where the original factory was in Ronda de Sant Antoni.

Chefs in action preparing signature tapas in the Tapas 24 bar.

The new creative *tapas*

The influence of high cuisine reached the world of tapas in the early 90s. The establishment of the long vertical tasting menus in restaurants led to a phenomenon that became known as "high cuisine in miniature". The revision of the world of tapas by El Bulli in 1989 incorporated new creativo concepts into the world of the snack and the tapa. In came liquid croquettes, shots of drinks, spoons, foams, the new texturisers, the innovative ways of cooking molluscs, the deconstructions...

In 1995 El Bulli opened the Talaia Mar in Barcelona, a restaurant with a philosophy close to tapas that was short-lived. It was run by Carlos Abellán and Marc Singla, the latter the author of the famous deconstructed potato omelette. Abellán continued serving creative tapas in the Comerç 24 restaurant and the Tapas 24 bar. Many other young chefs signed up for the new movement: Paco Santamaría, David Reartes, Dídac López... There was now no turning back. Classical tapas and catering would coexist forever with the vanguard.

Above, the version of Russian salad of the Cañete bar and the *patatas bravas* (spicy fried potatoes) of Tapas 24.

The city of cafés

There was a time, at the end of the 19th and early 20th century, in which the grand cafés of Barcelona competed in size, splendour and prestige with the most reputed establishments of the most important European capitals. Unfortunately, these establishments gradually closed and, in many cases, even the buildings that housed them were demolished. Nothing was preserved; only the memory remains and some, very few, old photographs that bear witness to the cheer and dynamism that the grand cafés of the past imprinted on a bourgeois society that wanted to turn them into veritable temples of the city's social life.

The first cafés in Barcelona appeared in the mid-18th century and were grouped in the Pla de les Comèdies, at the end of the La Rambla. They later proliferated in the Plaça Palau. Initially, the reputation of these premises was greatly questioned by the sanctimonious families of the city. Women did not usually go and entry was prohibited to minors who were not accompanied by an adult.

The oldest café in the city was the Café Caponata, opened in 1750 by an Italian restaurateur called Andreu Caponata.

The opening of the Cafè de les 7 Portes (1838), which still operates today as a restaurant, meant the confirmation of the new commercial and bourgeois image of the Plaça Palau. The luxurious spot had five rooms decorated with chandeliers, massive mirrors, marble tables, velvet divans, a billiard table and a piano.

On the left, Christmas greeting of El Gran Café (AHCB). Right: terrace of a café on La Rambla in the early 20th century.

Modernist interior and façade of the Casa Almirall bar-café in Carrer Joaquín Costa.

It was the first café that would incorporate gas lighting in 1844.

Among the most classical cafés of the 19th century stands out the spectacular Café de Cuyàs, in La Rambla, beside the Teatre Principal. Following in its steps were the Café de las Delicias, the Café Español and the Gran Café de España.

The list of the most emblematic cafés of the Modernist period would be interminable: Café del Liceo, Gran Café del Siglo XIX, the Café de las Cuatro Naciones…

The reputation of the cafés grew slowly during the mid-19th century and, gradually, left behind this notoriety of hideouts of crooks and idlers. Middle-class families began to frequent them, as

well as young people, who would often go in a group. It was the custom to go on Thursday afternoon or Sunday evening. In winter the *escalfeta* would be lit, a tin contraption that maintained the heat due to permanently lit hot coals with which they would usually light their cigarettes.

Many people went to the cafés to read the newspapers or ask for the "writing case", a set of paper, envelopes, inkpot and nib. Above all, however, the cafés became popular for their informal gatherings of all types and condition. In the Lion d'Or, in La Rambla, the literati and men of letters had traditionally met, just as Moratín documented in his correspondence.

Neither is it of any surprise that in Paral·lel there was a premises, surprisingly called La Tranquilidad, where anarchists met to debate their revolutionary ideas and plot their conspiracies which, by the way, did not forebode particularly tranquil times for the people of Barcelona.

View of the spectacular terrace of the now-vanished Café Español in Paral·lel.

The *cul de cafè* (the café dreg) was the name given to the people who were the centre of a gathering and were concerned with maintaining the discussion and enlivening it. In these gatherings, formalised groups took shape, which in many cases served as authentic centres of opinion formers in political, artistic, cultural, sporting or social matters.

At the beginning of the 20th century, the high society of the city started moving from the old centre towards the recently created Eixample district. Many cafés proliferated there too, some of which incorporated terraces on which it was very pleasant to sit and watch people passing by and enjoying the good weather.

The largest terrace in the city was, however, in the Café Español in Paral·lel and perhaps the most spectacular façade was shown off by the Cafè Torino, on the corner of Gran Via and Passeig de Gràcia.

Many of these establishments were elegantly decorated by the most noted painters and decorators of Catalan Modernism. Although the largest and most emblematic establishments from this period disappeared decades ago, the visitor could get an idea following a brief route around some small Modernist cafés in the city that would include the Café de la Ópera in La Rambla, the recently restored Café Vienés in Casa Fuster, Casa Almirall in Carrer Joaquín Costa or the old Cafè del Centre in Carrer Girona.

The Café del Centre is one of the few historic cafés that has survived. Above, façade of the Café Torino.

The world
of sweets

The confectionery of Barcelona is famous for being the best in the country. In the city's cake shops the visitor will find both respect for traditions and the technical refinement that converts the good into sublime. Just as occurred with the cuisine, Barcelona's confectionery always had a great admiration for what went on in the neighbouring country, France, and other European capitals. At the end of the 19th century, the drive of the new bourgeoisie enabled the cake shops to specialise in cake-making with products tra-

ditionally considered as more exclusive, such as fillings, cream or chocolate.

The visitor will be amazed by the number of specialities that follow one another in the windows of the cake shops throughout the year, in line with the calendar of festivals.

Thus, in the All Saints festivals, tradition requires that *panellets* are made, small sweets based on marzipan that can have the most diverse forms and flavours. The most appreciated *panellets* are, without doubt, the ones made with pine nuts, but a varied assortment is inexcusable without the coconut rocks, marzipan mushrooms or those flavoured with coffee, lemon or quince, among many others.

At Christmas many cake shops make their own *neules* (rolled wafer) and *torrons* (nougat) of egg yolk or marzipan. The classical *torrons* from Xixona can be found in specialised shops, some of which are in Carrer Portal de l'Àngel or Carrer Cucurulla, where long queues form. In summer, these establishments also enjoy great success as selling ice creams and tiger nut milk, *orxata*. Tiger nut milk is a whitish milky liquid that is obtained from a tiny and very tasty tuber: the tiger nut. The first *orxateria* in Barcelona was "El tío

In many confectioners in the city, classical confectionery coexists alongside vanguard sweets and cakes.

Sweet specialities of the Escribà confectioner's.

Nelo", opened in 1836 and active until 1890. The tiger nut milk of this establishment became as popular as the fritters that accompanied it.

On the sixth of January, the day on which the Kings from the Orient flood homes with gifts, it is the tradition to serve a *tortell de Reis* (ring-shaped cake) as dessert which can be presented filled with cream or marzipan.

The *bunyols*, fritters, plain and light or filled with cream, are another speciality typical of Barcelona cake-making and in Catalonia generally. Sometimes they are called *bunyols de Quaresma* (Lent) or *bunyols de l'Empordà* (the county) and are often aromatised with aniseed spirit and aniseed grains. They are fried in hot oil and later coated with lots of sugar before serving in the typical brown paper cones.

In March the *crema catalana* or *crema de Sant Josep* (Catalan custard) is an absoluter must and at Easter it is traditional to give as a present the spectacular *mones* or chocolate figures (see "The capital of chocolate").

The eve of Saint John's Day marks the beginning of the school summer holidays. It is celebrated with dances, bonfires, bangers, fireworks, cava and, above all, lots of confectionery *coques*, sweet flat cakes. The types of Saint John's Day *coques* on offer are very varied. The most typical ones usually contained glazed fruits, cream or pork scratching. The *coca de llardons* (pork scratching) can today be bought throughout the year in cake shops but, originally, it was a speciality typical of *dijous gras* (Fat Thursday) at carnival time.

The revolution of the desserts

The world of sweets could not be left out of the rethinking of criteria that the creative blooming of the Ferran Adrià phenomenon represented. In the mid-nineties, his brother Albert and the pastry cooks Oriol Balaguer and Jordi Butrón led a movement of renewal of the confectionery in restaurants from the vanguard approach. Until then, the dessert menu of a restaurant did not usually have a creative coherence with the rest of the menu. Cuisine and confectionery began to interact and share techniques, ingredients and creative processes.

The traditional confectionery of the cake shops, highly conditioned until then by the importance of the cut and transport of the classical cake, also began to apply some of the new approaches of the young and creative "dessert chefs". We cannot forget Xano Sagués, Carlos Mampel, Oriol Morató, Jordi Roca and many others who ensured that the movement would end up having an international impact.

Jordi Butrón giving classes at the Espai Sucre, school and restaurant of desserts.

The capital of chocolate

The citizens of Barcelona could not live without chocolate. It is no coincidence that for centuries the city's port was one of the main gateways to Europe of cocoa from America. Having become the fashionable drink among nobles and aristocrats, chocolate became absolutely essential in the high-standing meetings. This is certi-

fied by the Baron of Maldà in his engagement book, at the end of the 18th century, a genuine chronicler of the social life of Europe and confessed addict to mugs of chocolate.

Some notable families of the Catalan bourgeoisie made their fortunes at the end of the 19th century with the cocoa trade from the overseas colonies and its later transformation into chocolate. Casa Amatller, just beside Gaudí's Casa Batlló in Passeig de Gràcia, was entrusted to the architect Josep Puig i Cadafalch in 1898 by the businessman Antoni Amatller, owner of the famous chocolates that became popular due to its picture card collection. The gargoyles of the capitals on the stairway and in the dining room, work of the Modernist architect Eusebi Arnau, constitute a visual allegory about the cultivation and trade of cocoa and the elaboration of chocolate. The building can be visited and currently houses the prestigious Amatller Institute of Hispanic Art.

Continuing along Passeig de Gràcia upwards and crossing Diagonal, we reach the Jardinets de Gràcia, where Carrer Gran de Gràcia begins. On this corner is another of the most important Modernist buildings in the city, Casa Fuster, recently restored and converted into a luxury hotel. Before

Casa Amatller in Passeig de Gràcia belonged to a family of chocolate manufacturers.

the architect Lluís Domènech i Montaner planned this building as housing between 1908 and 1911, the site had housed the old Juncosa chocolate factory. The new hotel has also recovered the emblematic Café Vienés, which was situated in the building and formed a meeting point for intellectuals and artists until 1926.

We should also highlight the Riucord family in this section, a historic dynasty of chocolate makers and current owners of the Blasi make of chocolates.

Granges, farms, is the name given in the city to the establishments that, although having their origin in the sale of dairy products, ended up being famous for the great popularity of a very typi-

Hot chocolate with whipped cream, known as a *suís* (Swiss), is very popular in the *granges* (cafés) of Carrer Petritxol.

cal hot drink: the *suís*, the Swiss. In Barcelona, a *suís* is something more than a citizen of Switzerland. If you ask for a *suís* in a bar, a chocolate shop or *granja* they will bring you a mug of thick chocolate crowned by whipped cream. Although each district in the city has its own *granges*, enjoying a special prestige are the historic ones in Carrer Petritxol. We should also mention Granges Viader, where the most famous chocolate milkshake in the country was created: the Cacaolat.

If the visitor finds themselves wandering around the Gothic Quarter they simply must pay a visit to the Chocolatería Fargas, an emblematic spot founded in 1827 that still conserves its old cocoa grinding stone.

In 1950, the Nutrexpa company, founded in the district of Gràcia, launched Cola Cao into the market, a cocoa in powder that triumphed amongst the child public helped by its catchy advertising jingle that caused an uproar on the radio

Interior of the historic Fargas chocolate shop (1827), on the corner of Cucurulla and Pi streets.

of the time: "*I am that little black boy from tropical Africa who sang while growing…*"

Perhaps the moment when the visitor can confirm in a more specific way the fascination that the people of Barcelona have for chocolate is during the last days of the Easter holidays. Tradition demands that on Easter Monday godparents give their godchildren chocolate figures, known as *mones.* The shop windows of all the cake makers become authentic galleries of chocolate sculptures which range from the classical Easter eggs to the most famous children's personalities of that moment in time.

Another speciality that will amaze the visitor in the cake and chocolate shops of the city are the *catànies*, sweets based on almonds covered in white chocolate, milk and cocoa powder, typical of Vilafranca del Penedès.

It would be impossible to name here all the pastry and chocolate chefs who have achieved

Oriol Balaguer holds one of his original Easter eggs.

recognition in the world of chocolate. We should recall the figure of Josep Balcells, who appeared on the cover of National Geographic in 1984 with his chocolate figures. We must also mention Enric Rovira, among whose avant garde creations are bars of chocolate that reproduce the typical drawing of the paving stones of the city centre. And we cannot forget the Escribà family, or the Baixas dynasty, who in the seventies commercialised some famous boxes of chocolates inspired by the walking stick of Dalí.

Chocolate is an important ingredient of Catalan cuisine. It is used in savoury dishes, in sauce bases and spicy sauces, for dishes of rabbit, chicken, squid, prawns and lobster. Its importance is so great that the city has dedicated a large museum to it, a highly recommended visit.

Above, Christian Escribà recreating the skyscrapers of Manhattan in chocolate. Below, traditional Easter *mona,* chocolate figure.

La Boqueria: the cathedral of the senses

Markets are a reflection of the life of cities, the busy metaphor of the coming of the seasons, the cheer and sadness of our lifetime.

In the heart of the city, in the centre of La Rambla, the market of La Boqueria has always aroused the admiration of visitors and artists. Its colours, smells, flavours, noises and people have been reflected in the literature of Narcís Oller, Josep Maria de Sagarra, Mercè Rodoreda and Francisco Casavella, to mention just a few. Ma-

nuel Vázquez Montalbán defined La Boqueria as "the Cathedral of the Senses" and at the hand of Pepe Carvalho, his universal sceptical detective and gourmet, millions of readers around the world have passed through the narrow alleyways of the market in their imaginations, packed with fruit, vegetables, meat and fish.

Although there was always a market in the area, the modern history of La Boqueria dates back to the 1830s, when traders who sold in the centre of La Rambla were obliged to move to a new square in neoclassical style that had been built where there had been the convent of the discalced Carmelites, the church of Sant Josep and the site of the convent of Jerusalem, knocked down and expropriated after the sale of church lands, the law of Mendizábal.

The Plaça Sant Galdric, just behind the Palau de la Virreina, is the area of the peasant farm women, many of them daughters or granddaughters of the farmers from Baix Llobregat who came to sell their produce from the beginning of the last century. Installed in precarious stands in the open air and using the piled up fruit and vegetable boxes to place their scales, we are reminded that behind each piece of fruit or vegetable there

The columns in neoclassical style that surround the square are one of the identifying marks of the market.

The locally grown products, sold by the farm women from El Prat, coexist with the more exotic foods. This is the cosmopolitan character of La Boqueria

The people who work in the market are the veritable heart of La Boqueria. Above, Joan Bayén, the popular "Pinotxo"

is a human gesture, and effort linked to nature, the land and the whims of the weather.

Eating in the market is a unique experience. The photography of Joan Bayén "Pinocchio", dressed up in his characteristic fantasy waistcoat and bow tie, has gone all around the world. The bars of Mario and Ana, Quim and many others offer the freshest ingredients, at arm's length, freshly cooked and served to be tasted on a stool which for a few minutes becomes a veritable gourmets' throne.

In 2003 the Aula Gastronòmica was installed, a space designed to hold cooking courses, tasting sessions and workshops. One of the first directors was the late-lamented gastronome Llorenç Torrado, who lived right in front of the market, on the other side of La Rambla.

However, the most remembered personality of the market will always be Ramon Cabau. In some of the main stands his portrait is still conserved; he is recognised by the impossible moustache, the coloured bow tie and the straw hat. He was a man of extraordinary culture: lawyer, chemist and restaurateur. From his Agut d'Avinyó restaurant he spread the principles of Nouvelle Cuisine in Catalan cuisine and claimed the excel-

The colours of the fruit and vegetables ensure the visual spectacle following the chromatic variations of the vegetable calendar. Above, the famous mushroom stall of Llorenç Petràs.

lence of raw materials against banal products. In the early eighties he abandoned his restaurant to become a farmer in Canet de Mar. It was he who introduced to La Boqueria the first lettuce hearts, flowering courgettes, basil, dill, spring onion, pea

flower or violet... in a period in which these ingredients were very difficult to find.

In 1982 he decided to put an end to his life in a very unconventional way. Like every day, Ramon Cabau went to his beloved La Boqueria market

and gave a flower from his orchard to each one of his suppliers and friends. Later that day, he swallowed a capsule of cyanide and died in the arms of his friend, Llorenç Petràs. It was a gastronomic suicide, a declaration of love, romantic and desperate, to the most beautiful market in the world.

The love for gastronomy and market cuisine is summed up in the fascinating story of Ramon Cabau. Above, the Soley vegetable stall still has a portrait of the much-loved gastronome on display.

The markets of the city

The first documents relating to the markets of Barcelona date back to the 10th century. The first market open was situated outside the wall that surrounded the old city, where the Plaça de l'Àngel is today. In the Middle Ages, El Born functioned as an open market and was the centre where they held the jousts of the nobility and the religious and leisure festivals, such as the Carnival.

The first covered market in the city was that of Santa Caterina (1844). This market was built on the site where there had been an old convent and the church of Santa Caterina, burnt down in 1835. The roof has recently been reformed in a spectacular way by the architects Enric Miralles and Benedetta Tagliabue.

Above, the attractive roof of the Santa Caterina market aims to pay homage to the richness of colours of the foods on the stalls. On the right, the Galvany market.

It was the mayor Rius i Taulet who promoted the expansion of the markets in the new Barcelona, such as those of Sant Antoni (1882), Barceloneta (1884), Concepció and Hostafrancs (1888), Clot and Poblenou (1889) and Abaceria Central in Gràcia (1892).

Modernism would leave its mark, characterised by the use of iron and metal, in many markets, in the image of the pioneering Les Halles in Paris. El Born was the first market built with this Modernist conception on the same spot where

the old medieval market had been. In 1888 the Mercat de la Llibertat was opened in the old Vila de Gràcia village. At the beginning of the century markets were created in the neighbouring towns that would soon be annexed to the city as districts: Sarrià (1911), Sants (1913), Sant Andreu (1923) and Galvany (1927). In recent years a renovation process has been under way to give them better infrastructures and services.

Just 10 kilometres from the centre of Barcelona is Mercabarna, the food distribution centre

The Sant Antoni market is one of the most emblematic in the city. It was opened in 1882.

that concentrates the wholesale markets (Fruit and vegetables, Fish and Flowers) and the Barcelona slaughterhouse, as well as 450 companies of preparation, commerce, distribution, import and export of fresh foods. In its precinct, of 90 ha, there are a total of 700 companies.

Located strategically in the centre of a network of communications –close to the terminal of the international airport, the sea port, the railway station and with a direct connection to the main motorways , Mercabarna supplies more than 10 million people and is a benchmark market around the world

Photos of day-to-day activities in the Mercabarna central wholesale market.

Barceloneta: the city in the sea

For many years, practically until the dramatic transformation that the city underwent due to the holding of the 1992 Olympic Games, it was said that Barcelona lived with its back to the sea. It was true, with the exception of a very charismatic district that was founded and grew with a marked port, seafaring and Mediterranean character: Barceloneta.

When in 1714 Felipe V razed the district of La Ribera to build the fortification of Ciutadola, many families from the area took refuge in the huts that they built on the beach. With the passing of time, these early huts would end up being inhabited by fishermen and coalmen or used as warehouses for port tools.

The big increase in immigration to Barcelona, still a small walled city with an overwhelming demographic density, resulted in the birth of the district on the land that had been gained from the sea to build the port's sheltering dock. Initially, this new area was known as "the District of the Beach" although it ended up being known by the popular diminutive of "Barceloneta".

The closeness of the sea has marked the character of Barceloneta, one of the most charismatic districts of the city. On demolishing the old *tinglados* (huts), the district recovered the sea views.

In the background the Sant Sebastià tower, which since 1931 has connected Barceloneta with the Montjuïc mountain via a cable car.

Narrow streets, small houses, lively squares… the life in Barceloneta has a lively and Mediterranean emphasis, of people who live facing the sea, many of them still descendants of sailors, fishermen and dockers.

Some taverns called *pudes* proliferated on the La Riba wharf in the mid-19th century where one could eat, drink, and play cards amid the smoke of smuggled tobacco and smells of fried fish. Later on, in the nineteen-twenties, some fishermen began to assemble huts on the beach, where they cooked the small fish that the owners of the boats shared out with their sailors. These precarious eating places, which were installed in summer and taken down in winter, were very popular with the people of Barcelona, who came on the trolley bus to the historic bathing clubs of the area. As the years went by, they went from being provisional snack bars to becoming authentic restaurants with lots of tables placed on the

Barceloneta has been able to conserve a very personal identity of its own. The popular character of the district can be felt strolling around its narrow and welcoming streets.

sandy beach. The last of these establishments was knocked down in 1994.

Taverns and restaurants also proliferated in the interior part of the district. In some places the cooking was done in a family atmosphere to feed the sailors and workers of the area. In other bodegas it was allowed to take your own food, offering the sale of wine or vermouth in exchange for the use of the tables. It was in the most festive taverns where the mythical flamenco dancer Carmen Amaya made her debut, having been born in the neighbouring Somorrostro, a district of huts on the beach, today disappeared.

The last two decades have dramatically changed the urban landscape of the district. The beach snack bars have been relocated and they have knocked down the "sheds" or warehouses of Passeig Joan de Borbó, returning the sea view to the district. As testimony to that past the building that today houses the History of Catalonia Museum still stands.

At the Barceloneta exchange the sale of fresh fish takes place daily. The licence corresponds to the Fishermen's Brotherhood of Barcelona. The city has a fleet of more than forty fishing boats, mainly seine fishing and trawling.

Tapas with a seafaring flavour are mandatory in the many bars and restaurants. The fishmongers maintain the seafaring spirit of the district.

The arrival of the boats to the exchange is a daily liturgy.
In many cases, the fish goes directly to the restaurants
in the district.

Two auctions take place each day. The auction of the seine fishing fleet begins at 7 a.m., above all for blue fish: sardines, mackerel, anchovies and horse mackerel, among others. At 4.45 p.m. the afternoon session is held, in which the trawling fish are auctioned: prawns, Dublin Bay prawns, hake, red mullet, monkfish...

To help in identifying the fish and seafood caught by the Barcelona fishing fleet, a promotional campaign has been started based on the creation of the collective brand "Peix de la Barceloneta".

The cuisine of the district has been shaped with these ingredients provided by the massive larder of the sea. The fish recipes of the Catalan coast have been gradually fused with the dishes brought by all those people who came from other parts of Spain, especially Andalucía and Galicia. Fish stews, rice dishes, paellas and noodles, seafood, blue fish and rock fish... But perhaps the most representative dish of Barceloneta is the *bomba*. It is a meatball made of mashed potato filled with mincemeat and then fried. This delicious snack, so much loved and so popular, was invented in one of the most charismatic spots in the district: La Cova Fumada, a pleasant bodega

The seafaring flavour of Barceloneta is reflected in a very characteristic cuisine of its own that is supplied by the grand larder of the sea. On the right, the fish auction.

La Cova Fumada is a very emblematic restaurant that still conserves the flavour of bygone times.

situated in Plaça Poeta Boscà that still maintains the flavour of a now-past era. The new times of design and urban cosmetics of Barceloneta have not yet reached the headquarters of this *bomba*, the only peaceful "bomb" in the world.

Peas of Llavaneres

They say that the first testimony about these delicious and highly regarded peas was in the book *Diario de los viajes y hechos en Cataluña,* written by Francisco Zamora in the 17th century. Its cultivation was intensified in the nineteen-thir-

Sweet, large and very tasty, the Llavaneres pea enjoys great prestige among gourmets. Of low return economically, it is a product that reaches high prices in the market.

ties and was even exported to France. The truth is that today there are very few farmers from the county who cultivate them, generally along with broad beans, tomatoes and a few other vegetables. The main producers are in Cabrera de Mar, Argentona and Alella, among other towns.

The pea of Llavaneres or Maresme pea, whatever one wants to call it, requires some special care and its cultivation represents an almost ar-

tisanal effort which, naturally, is reflected in the price. Its main enemies are the inclement weather (wind, ice, drought…) and the greedy *tudons* (wood pigeons), which can raze the plants in just a few hours.

Seeding is done during October in siliceous and sandy soil. The seed is produced by the farmers themselves. In the past only one or, sometimes, two, harvests were obtained. Today, the season has been lengthened from January to April, the last two months being the most productive.

The pea of Llavaneres is known, above all, for its delicate and sweet flavour. It was in the mythical Ca la Petra restaurant where its fame crossed the frontiers of the county spreading throughout Catalonia. Petra Lafarga popularised the recipe of *pèsols ofegats* (sautéed peas), perhaps the simplest and best way of tasting these delicate vegetables. Later, the sisters Paquita and Lolita Reixach, from the Hispània restaurant in Arenys de Mar, converted some dishes such as peas with blood sausage into the most emblematic ones of their prestigious establishment. The current top chef of the Maresme, Carme Ruscalleda, also cooks them with great care in her Sant Pau restaurant in Sant Pol de Mar.

Some people still call them by their popular name of *els pèsols de la floreta* (the peas of the flower). In fact they should be called *pèsols garrofals* (carob tree peas), since it is a specific variety that adapted to the carob tree fields of the area. Unfortunately, since its cultivation does not reach a specific number of hectares, it has been unable to achieve a Denomination of Origin certificate that protects its quality.

Every year, during April, in Sant Andreu de Llavaneres the *Festa del Pèsol* (Pea Festival) is hold. They organise events, tasting sessions and diverse cooking demonstrations in which the local restaurants take part. Other neighbouring towns, such as Mataró, Cabrils and Vilassar de Mar, have also started organising gastronomic days to pay homage to this small and sweet delicacy of the Maresme.

This variety of pea, also known as *pèsol garrofal*, grows on high bushes that may reach two metres in height.

It is one of the smallest Denomination of Origin areas in the country. The wines of Alella have had to fight against heavy urban speculation.

D.O.
Alella wines

Situated just ten kilometres from Barcelona, the historic vineyards of Alella could be considered as urban vineyards. However, this closeness to the city is also the cause of the strong speculative pressure that they have experienced and which has placed their survival in danger. The cultivated area of the vineyards has dwindled spectacularly in just a few decades due to the attractiveness of the land, ideal for building residential areas with wonderful views of the Mediterranean Sea and a few minutes by car from the city centre. Nevertheless, despite the overwhelming drive of urban development, the wines of Alella have been able to keep a millenary agricultural tradition alive with a commitment to quality. It is a great example of tenacity and resistance in a very unequal battle.

The qualities of the wines of Alella are documented from Roman times. They were known as *Laietan* wines and their virtues were already extolled by the historians Pliny and Martialis. In the Middle Ages, the area of Alella was still the main

many winemakers who were forced to sell their land. The vineyards were replanted with American stock and in 1894 the first harvest of these grafted stocks was achieved. The wines of Alella soon recovered their market and their reputation among the Barcelona upper classes. During the first two decades of the 20th century their prestige became international with large exports to overseas markets in Cuba, Chile, Bolivia, Peru, Argentina and New York.

Created in 1953, the Denomination of Origin "Ví d'Alella" is currently one of the smallest on the Iberian peninsula, although its specific weight in Catalan winemaking is still very important and illustrates a courageous commitment to modernity and quality.

The climate in the area is Mediterranean, rainfall is no more than 600 mm and the average annual temperature is 15 degrees centigrade. Every plot has its own microclimate based on factors such as the orientation, the closeness to the sea and the woods or the slope of the land. We can divide the vineyards into two sides; the eastern-facing slopes, majestically situated opposite the sea, and the slopes facing the west, sheltered from the sea breeze and with less humidity. Some new vine-

supplier of quality wines to the city of Barcelona. They were wines that were always praised for their freshness and intrinsic Mediterranean character.

The devastating plague of phylloxera at the end of the 19th century caused the ruin of

The white wines of Alella have a special reputation. Reds, rosés and cavas are also produced.

yards have been planted in the higher areas, with a fresher climate at some 150 metres in altitude.

The main variety is the autochthonous *Pansa Blanca*, although the *Macabeu, Parellada* and *Chardonnay* grapes are also grown. The wines of Alella are known above all for the delicate, Mediterranean and calm character of its whites. The reds are also of great quality and are made with varieties such as *Garnatxa negra, Merlot, Syrah* and *Cabernet Sauvignon*, mainly.

The Denomination of Origin covers the wines produced in the districts of Alella, Argentona, Cabrils, El Masnou, La Roca del Vallès, Martorelles, Montornès del Vallès, Montgat, Òrrius, Premià de Dalt, Premià de Mar, Santa Maria de Martorelles, Sant Fost de Campcentelles, Teià, Tiana, Vallromanes, Vilanova del Vallès and Vilassar de Dalt.

Cherries from Baix Llobregat

The vineyard huts among the cherry fields remind us that, before the phylloxera, many parts of the mountains of Baix Llobregat were covered with vines. The crops and the landscape changed dramatically and today would be difficult to recognise, above all when spring comes and the cherry trees

are covered with delicate pale pink flowers, a symbol of the regeneration of life for the Japanese and a tree par excellence for people in love.

The county of Baix Llobregat produces half of all the cherries eaten in Catalonia. The first and most traditional variety is the *Burlat*, very sweet and a wine red colour. The *Starky Hardy* has also made its presence felt, juicy and more resistant to the spring rainfall. There are hundreds of varieties that can be selected by differ-

Cherry production in Baix Llobregat is focused, above all, in the mountainous areas of the Montbaig-Montpedrós sierras.

ent criteria: flavour, sweetness or acidity, calibre, resistance...

The season is very short, from the end of April until mid-July. Several towns such as Sant Climent, Santa Coloma de Cervelló, Torrelles de Llobregat or El Papiol dress themselves up each year between May and early June to welcome the festivals dedicated to the cherry. Activities of all kinds are organised: tasting sessions, competitions, gastronomic demonstrations, firework displays... There is even a curious competition that consists of spitting out the stones as far as possible. Without doubt, cherries –red, tasty and playful– serve many purposes.

The climate and land of Baix Llobregat are ideal for growing cherries. More than one hundred different varieties are grown.

Artichokes from El Prat

Barcelona is the only Mediterranean metropolis with wetlands right by the gateway to the metropolitan area. The Delta del Llobregat is a protected natural space, of great ecological value, situated in the middle of the migratory route of birds from the north of Europe to Africa. It is made up of an extensive area that occupies 98 km^2 between the massif of El Garraf, Montjuïc and the gorge of Sant Andreu de la Barca in the north. It is one of the richest agricultural areas of the Mediterranean. The protected natural spaces coexist with the cultivated land, urban and industrial areas and infrastructures such as the airport of Barcelona.

The agricultural area can be visited in organised trips that explain all the characteristics of its production and its culinary uses.

The artichoke of El Prat grows in this humid, saline setting with a temperate climate, and has a characteristic sweet flavour. The closeness of the city is also an important qualitative factor, since it appears in the markets in a tenderer, fresher and more hydrated condition. The season lasts from November until June.

The Agrarian Park of Baix Llobregat organises routes to discover how the artichoke of El Prat is grown. In these guided trips we visit the produc-

tion fields in the company of a farmer and there are tasting and cooking workshops to discover the excellent qualities of the product. It is an initiative promoted by a group of farmers who aim to achieve a Protected Geographical Indication from the European Union.

The Delta del Llobregat and its wetlands is a protected and unique space of great ecological value.

Blue-footed chicken from El Prat

The slate blue of its feet was the reason why the popular name was given to this unique and unusual breed of chicken, very abundant in the county of Baix Llobregat.

The chickens of El Prat are raised with sufficient space to have freedom of movement. This means that their meat is tastier, firmer and with little fat.

The characteristic and attractive colours of the feathers of these birds, with shades that tend towards reddish, make them easily identifiable in the market. In the case of the roosters, the colour is brighter, especially the neck and back feathers, which shine as if they had been lacquered with varnish.

The chickens from El Prat –or blue-footed chickens– are greatly appreciated by the most demanding gourmets due to the quality and fla-

History tells us that domestic chickens reached Europe during Neolithic times from China and south-east Asia. It was the Greeks who introduced them to the lands of the Mediterranean basin. Many testimonies recall that, at the end of the 19th century, the farmers and first poultry breeders from El Prat del Llogregat, spontaneously selected and improved a type of rustic Mediterranean chicken, leading to the traits and characteristics that would eventually define the Catalan breed of El Prat. In fact, it is one of the breeds of poultry that has survived until our times without having been crossbred with other hybrid breeds. These morphological characteristics have always differentiated these blue-footed chickens and have provided them with the approval of the most demanding palates.

Faced with the mass production that poultry breeding has experienced in recent years, the raising of chickens in El Prat continues to be very carefully monitored. They are birds raised in liberty and in chicken coops in which the number of eight animals per square metre cannot be surpassed. Eighty per cent of their food consists of cereals and the minimum period of growth is 90 days.

vour of their meat. They belong to the Catalan breed of El Prat and in 1987 the Generalitat (autonomous government) awarded a General Denomination accrediting the quality of the chickens and capons bred in El Prat de Llobregat and in the municipal districts of Castelldefels, Cornellà de Llobregat, Gavà, Sant Boi de Llobregat, Sant Feliu de Llobregat, Viladecans and Santa Coloma de Cervelló.

They have a Protected Geographical Indication, being the only chickens from the Iberian peninsula with this specific denomination regulated by the European Union to protect high quality food. As well as their peculiar morphological characteristics, it is easy to recognise them in the market as they reach the sales points with a label of the Regulatory Council that identifies them.

Their meat is very tasty, with hardly any fat, and they require much longer cooking times than commercially bred chickens. This is why their consumption is associated with special occasions, celebrations and, very specifically, they have become an essential ingredient on the tables at Christmas in the neighbouring counties.

Every December the Poultry Fair of El Prat is held, an annual event that coincides with the days before the Christmas holidays and which has become an important boost for the recovery and diffusion of these chickens and capons. With a turnout of the public of approximately 100,000 visitors and an average of 60 producers, in just three days some 2,500 adult birds are sold at the fair for consumption as well as 1,000 chicks. The demand surpasses the supply on these dates.

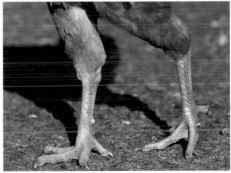

The slate blue colour of their feet, their reddish feathers and the large toothed crest are the most identifiable traits of this breed.

D.O. Cava

Manuel Vázquez Montalbán said in a very poetic way that *"cava is the open door for the spirit to escape from"*. The popularity of sparkling wines –whose bubbles overflowed over the glasses, produced a pleasant tickle on the palate and cheered the heart–, dates back to texts as classical as Virgil's *Aeneid*.

In Catalonia Francesc Eiximenis already spoke of the *"saltants i formigalejants"* (restless and tingling) wines in the 14th century. The great prestige acquired by champagne due to the improvements introduced by the Benedictine friar Don Pierre Perignon made winemakers from all over Europe interested in its commercialisation and soon established itself in the most elitist social circles as a drink of great prestige.

The main varieties of grapes used for cava are macabeu, xarel·lo and parellada. On the right, the minimum ageing time is nine months.

In the history of Catalan cava we should mention two pioneering experts: Agustí Vilaret, producer from Blanes and grand theoretician of the *méthode champenoise* and Luis Justo Villanueva, professor of chemistry at the Agricultural Institute of Sant Isidre. Two of Villanueva's most advanced students –Miquel Esquirol and Josep Raventós, from winemaking families of the Penedès region– began to experiment together in the basement of a flat in Barcelona and, later, in the family home of Can Codorníu, in Sant Sadurní d'Anoia. The first Catalan champagne –before being called *cava*– was made in 1872 and commercialised by Codorníu in 1879. They sold seventy-two boxes and it was so successful that many winemakers from the area began to produce the new wine applying the knowledge developed by these pioneers.

The dramatic transformation of the vineyard of Penedès due to the phylloxera plague meant the replacement of red varieties for classical white grapes used for the production of cava: Macabeo, Xarel·lo and Parellada. To these have been later added other varieties of diverse origins such as Chardonnay, Subirat or Malvasia Riojana, and the red Garnatxa, Monastrell, Pinot Noir and Trepat, the latter variety authorised only in the production of rosé cavas.

The environs of Sant Sadurní d'Anoia are known as cava country. Most of the cava protected by the D.O. is produced here, although the geographical area protected is very large and covers three counties of Catalonia and towns in La Rioja, Aragón, Navarra, the Basque Country and Extremadura.

The production of cava requires a singular fermentation process. Through gentle pressing a must is obtained with which the "base wine" is made. After clarification, the fermentation process is started with selected yeasts and strict control of the temperatures to be able to obtain the utmost from the fruity characteristics of each grape variety used. These different wines are mixed in a carefully designed *coupage* to define the singular personality that each producer wants.

The traditional method or *champenoise* begins with the first fermentation, an operation that consists of bottling the wine with the addition of a mix-

Catalan cava began to be made in the late-19th century following the champagne method.
Its success was immediate and it became a drink associated with celebrations and festive occasions.

ture of yeasts and sugar which, on fermenting, will produce the characteristic froth of the cava.

The "rhyme" –or frothing– takes place in underground cellars, while the bottles rest horizontally, in a damp atmosphere and a temperature that does not surpass 15° C, for a maturing period of at least nine months. In this second fermentation in the bottle, the bubbles of carbonic gas gradually dissolve into the wine and, together with the yeasts, give the cava its peculiar aroma and flavour.

The ageing process can last as long as the producer wants. A cava with the Gran Reserva label must have an ageing process of at least 30 months.

Once the ageing process is completed, the deposits from the second fermentation that remain in the bottle must be eliminated. To do this, a daily "riddling" is carried out of the bottles in the "desks". This involves giving the bottle a quarter turn with a small vibratory movement,

On the left, different moments in the production of cava.
Above, the rotating movement of the bottles called "riddling".
Below, three moments of "disgorging".

From then on, the quantity of liquid rests and the "expedition spirit" is added, a mixture of wine and sugar, according to the type of cava required: Brut Nature (without the addition of sugar), Extra Brut (up to 6 grams of sugar per litre), Brut (up to 15 g), Extra Sec (between 12 and 20 g), Sec (between 17 and 35 g), Semisec (between 33 and 50 g) and Dolç (more than de 50 g). The cava is sealed again with a cork top. The miracle is ready.

also varying minimally the degree of inclination. Then, placing the bottles upside down, the "disgorging" takes place, uncorking the bottles so that, with a small amount of froth coming out, the residual deposits are removed.

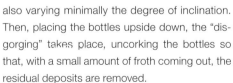

The liquid lost during the "disgorging" stage is replaced with a mixture of wine and sugar: the "expedition spirit".

barcelona_cuisine

Places
with flavour

01_Quimet & Quimet
02_Oriol Balaguer
03_Cafés El Magnífico
04_Escribà
05_La casa del Bacalao
06_Dry Martini
07_Casa Gispert
08_Fleca Fortino
09_Monvínic
10_Caelum
11_Queviures Múrria
12_Museum of the chocolate
13_Granja Viader
14_Horchatería Sirvent
15_Vila Viniteca
16_El Xampanyet

Quimet & Quimet

In the heart of the Poble-sec district, a few steps away from Paral·lel, we find this tiny spot run by the fourth generation of the Pérez family. It seems like a miracle that, in such a tiny space, there is such a varied and abundant delicatessen on offer: cured meats, hams, cheeses, salted, smoked, pickled and tinned seafood, –some of which can be ordered even with extras– and an impressive selection of wines and beers that pack the walls of the premises, giving it a certain air of a museum for gourmets. The establishment opened in 1914, as a bodega dedicated to the production and sale of wine. The brother and sister Quim and Joana Pérez and Quim's mother, Carmen Estal, are very clear: they are committed to quality and want to turn it into an authentic "cocktail bar of conserves". It is an absolute must to taste their personal creations: the mussel tapa, crystallised tomatoes and oregano; smoked salmon with yoghurt and truffle honey; medlar in syrup with Torta del Casar cheese...

c/ Poeta Cabanyes, 25
Tel: 93 442 31 42

Oriol Balaguer

After training as a pastry chef, he worked for a long time with Ferran and Albert Adrià, leading a revolution that ended breaking the frontiers between the sweet and the savoury and introducing new techniques and ingredients into the world of confectionery. The Oriol Balaguer shop seems more like a jeweller's than a confectioner-chocolate shop. With a stunning design, it makes 33 m² serve as a shop window for the most modern tendencies in the world of confectionery. There are no counters, only shelves and a large glass table that is the display section. The concept-cake is on show in a refrigerated glass cabinet, a unique creation that is renewed each month. The classical brioche products (plum-cakes, croissants, financiers...) coexist with the vanguard.

Among the most successful specialities feature the Paradigma cake with eight different textures of chocolate, and the chocolates in the form of a cocoa bean with unusual flavours: yuzu, toasted maize, Peta Zeta sherbet, wasabi... The aim? To thrill.

Pl. Sant Gregori
Taumaturgy, 2
Tel: 93 201 18 46

Cafés El Magnífico

Here every type of coffee is treated as if it were "a unique, precious and exclusive jewel". Salvador Sans belongs to the third generation of a dynasty of coffee roasters and has turned his company into the number one roaster of the country. It was he who introduced, for the first time in the country, high quality coffees such as "Jamaica Blue Mountain", "Puerto Rico Yauco Selecto" or "Hawaii Kona". One of the keys of his business consists of travelling around the five continents to meet the farmers "in situ". He has thus become a standard bearer of sustainable commerce and defends ethical and ecological rules, which have an effect on the quality of life of the coffee-producing communities and, finally, the quality of the coffee too. They have more than 30 types of coffee, the best ones in the world, which they roast in small quantities to preserve their freshness and the nuances of flavour, aroma and acidity that make them unique. They also sell ecologically grown and biodynamic coffees.

c/ Argenteria, 64
Tel: 93 319 39 75

Escribà

Antoni Escribà (1931-2004) was a very popular and much-loved character. He was considered the "magician of chocolate" and his spectacular Easter *mones* –the traditional chocolate figures, typical of Easter– delighted several generations of children.

His three sons have succeeded him: Christian, Joan and Jordi. The Escribà dynasty began on the premises of number 546 Gran Via, with a bakery opened in 1906 which later became a cake shop. In 1986 the family bought the premises in La Rambla, where the Casa Figueras had been, and with excellent taste, they left the Modernist decoration of the place intact. The Escribà family slogan is "We don't only make cakes, we create illusions".

They organise unique and personalised events full of fantasy. The sweet imagination of Christian Escribà has toured the world with his successful edible jewels, in the form of caramel rings.

La Rambla, 83
Tel: 93 301 60 27

La casa del Bacalao

Cod has always been one of the signs of identity of the city's cuisine. The writer Josep Pla stated that, in Barcelona, the cod was magnificent and he attributed this to the skill of the shopkeepers in desalting and preparing it. In this central establishment, close to the commercial street Portal de l'Àngel, there had previously been another cod shop. In 1979, the current owners opened the establishment and, since then, have been committed to achieving the utmost quality in the product. The cod comes from the Faroe Isles in the North Atlantic. The key to success seems to be the way of cutting the cod, using traditional methods, today almost forgotten. As well as the fillets, centres and top sections, here you can find tails, bellies and napes. Other much-sought after parts are the jaws and the entrails, which provide all its gelatinous aspect to many traditional recipes. You can also get pre-cooked dishes such as croquettes, cod fritters and *brandada*, a cod mix.

c/ Comtal 8
Tel: 93 301 65 39

Dry Martini

Since he opened his first premises –the first Gimlet cocktail bar, in December 1979–, Javier de las Muelas has become one of the most important referents in the international cocktail culture, constantly committed to innovation, design and sophistication. The Dry Martini is an emblematic spot of the Barcelona night. The atmosphere is welcoming and warm. The bar is made of classic wood and the walls are decorated with vanguard paintings. In 2002 he wanted to pay homage to the shebeens of prohibition in the United States and opened the Speakeasy, a small camouflaged restaurant inside the cocktail bar. Among his most famous creations feature the Spoon Martinis –edible cocktails that are eaten with a spoon– and the new creative range that includes flowers and vegetables, such as the Moshisho –a remake of the mojito with green and brown leaves of perilla– or the Carnivore, –a mixture of fruit juices with grape liquor and Sichuan Buttons electric flowers–.

c/ Aribau, 162-166
Tel: 93 217 50 72

Maestros Tostadores
Casa Gispert

On entering through the doorway you will get the sensation of having entered the set of a Christmas tale. Time seems to have stood still in this delightful spot with its old wood-fired oven, wooden shelves, hundred-year-old counter and straw baskets full of still smoking roasted dried fruits... From the town of Centelles, doctor Gispert bought this premises in 1851 for his sons to set up a warehouse of colonial products –coffee, cocoa, saffron, tea...– which they commercialised in bulk. Later, they specialised in the roasting of coffee and dried fruits. Among the varied offer feature the roasted dried fruits, coffees, teas, infusions and a careful selection of chocolates, honeys, jams and preserves. They also supply cavas and sweet wines, different types of salt and sugar, jams and all types of delicatessen food. They have a wide range of Christmas and gift hampers

c/ Sombrerers, 23
Tel: 93 319 75 35

Fleca Fortino

PAN COCIDO CON LEÑA

PANS INTEGRALS

NOSTRA DE
TORRADES

CUIT AMB LLENYA

Fleca Fortino

This is the ideal place for those looking for real bread, made in the traditional way in one of the very few wood-fired ovens remaining in Barcelona. Faced with the banality of bread that has meant the massive appearance of bakeries with very aggressive commercial criteria, Fortino is an example of resistance of the small bakery committed to quality and respect for traditional production. The result is a solid bread, with lots of flavour and which lasts for up to five days. Moreover, they have been able to adapt to the new times with traditional production of wholemeal breads in which they use one hundred per cent wholemeal flour, without mixtures, and including products such as organic spelt, quinoa or spirulina in some of its breads. We must also highlight their wholemeal biscuits and tea cakes, products without wheat, classic and wholemeal cakes, pizza bases and products with organic flours, among many others.

c/ Travessera de Gràcia, 145
Tel: 93 237 38 73

Monvínic

The best wine bar in the world? The idea is, quite simply, amazing. Sergi Ferrer Salat opened this spectacular space, designed by Alfons Tost, in 2008. The bodega, with an extensive and very carefully chosen selection of thousands of wines from around the world, is permanently updated and is the authentic heart of the establishment. Additionally, you can visit the centre of specialised documentation or take part in presentations, tasting sessions and conferences. Each day the wine bar offers a selection of some thirty wines in glasses or half-glasses, accompanied by tapas inspired by traditional Catalan cuisine. The diner can consult an impressive wine list with the help of a PC tablet to comfortably browse through the bodegas, production areas, grape varieties... In the culinary space the team of sommeliers suggests the best combinations with the traditionally-based cuisine, elegantly modernised.

c/ Diputació, 249
Tel: 93 272 61 87

Caelum

Get ready to taste the authentic bocados de cardenal... Gemma Arruga and Conchita Mont decided to travel all over Spain visiting convents and monasteries and selecting the best specialities made traditionally by the monks and nuns. This is how Caelum was formed, a lovely shop in a quiet street in the Gothic Quarter in which there are many antique shops. Suspiros de monja, tocinillos de cielo, yemas de Santa Teresa, Huesos de San Expedito, Rosas de Santa Catalina, lunitas, jams, preserves, jellies, liquors... Divine temptations that tempt one to commit a sin. The basements of the cosy premises are old vaulted Gothic baths that date back to the 14th century. At the tables you can taste the specialities of the nuns while listening to classical music or Gregorian chants. Everything here is an invitation to approach life with a heavenly calm. And in fact *caelum* means heaven in Latin...

**c/ de la Palla, 8
Tel: 93 302 69 93**

Queviures Múrria

Restless, erudite and friendly, Joan Múrria is a charming character in the gastronomic sphere of the city. He belongs to several guilds and associations linked to the world of wine, cava, cheese and gastronomy in general and has contributed regularly in the media as a promoter of natural, innovative products of the highest quality. For all his work, in 2001 he received the Medal of Honour of Barcelona awarded by the City Council.

The Colmado Múrria, founded in 1898, is a visit not to be missed on the tourist routes to discover the Modernist premises of the Eixample district. Its stock is based on delicatessen foods and personalised service. It provides gastronomic advice services. Among its specialities feature the impressive assortment of cheeses, foie gras, Iranian caviar and from the Vall d'Aran, Iberian hams, cured meats for celiacs, oils, wines, cavas and whiskies.

c/ Roger
de Llúria, 85
Tel: 93 215 57 89

Museum
of chocolate

Located in the building of the old convent of Sant Agustí in El Born, the Museum of Chocolate was created in 2000 by the Confectionery Guild of Barcelona. With more than 600 m² of space, the museum is divided into different areas in which there is an informative tour through the history and myths of cocoa, its Mayan and Aztec origins and its arrival in Europe. It also has exhibition spaces of old tools and machines from old Catalan chocolate factories. The tradition of the mones and Easter eggs occupies a leading place with massive sculptures in chocolate. The museum organises many courses, workshops and demonstra-tions, as well as guided visits for schools and groups. Family activities and children's festivals are very popular in which children cook, learn and end up tasting delicious things made with chocolate they have prepared themselves.

c/ Comerç, 36
Tel: 93 268 78 78

Granja Viader

Get ready to travel in time. In 1870 a dairy was opened here and at these tables sat figures such as Picasso or Father Cinto Verdaguer. Marc and Matilde Viader, great grandparents of the current owners, ran this place from 1904. The recipes are still the same as then and the milk and eggs still come from the farms of Cardedeu, just as in the past. The Granja Viader was the origin of the most important dairy centres in the country, Letona, linked to the family until the 1970s. This was also where, in 1931, the recipe for Cacaolat, the popular chocolate milkshake, was invented in 1931, which Joan Viader created with a Hungarian chemist. Among the specialities of the house are the hot chocolate and cream *suïssos*, whipped cream, Mallorca milk, Catalan custard, *mel i mató* (cottage cheese with honey), cottage cheese crème caramel, junket... They also have a wide variety of traditionally-made cakes and assortments of Catalan and Iberian cheeses and cured meats.

c/ Xuclà, 4-6
Tel: 93 318 34 86

Orxateria Turroneria
Sirvent

Tiger nut milk has become a widely accepted drink in Barcelona since the faraway times in which the now disappeared Orxatería del Tío Nelo made it immensely popular among the people of Barcelona in the mid-19th century.

Many foreign visitors are still pleasantly surprised to discover the excellent properties of this refreshing drink made from the tuber of a plant called tiger nut (*Cyperus sculentus*).

Casa Sirvent is famous for serving the best tiger nut milk in Barcelona. Located very close to the historic market of Sant Antoni, this establishment is recognisable from a distance due to the long queues and double-parked cars in front of its doors.

In 1920, Mr Tomás Sirvent Planelles, producer of *torrons*, nougats, in Xixona, settled in Barcelona and, since then, the family surname has been associated with the manufacture of tiger nut milk and traditionally-made nougats of the utmost quality.

c/ Parlament, 56
Tel: 93 441 27 20

Vila Viniteca

Very close to Santa María del Mar, in the heart of the La Ribera district, is this temple of wine. Quim Vila has wisely converted the family business –a small grocer's founded by his grandfather in 1932– into an obligatory reference for any lover of the city. A team of highly qualified professionals advise the visitor. The offer is impressive and includes some 7,000 wines, cavas, champagnes and spirits from all over the world. In a nearby classroom courses are given and tasting sessions are organised of the highest level. Next to the Viniteca is the grocer's that is run by Quim's sister, Eva, a grand specialist in select cheeses. Here you can buy and taste the best jams, Iberian hams, cured meats and gourmet products. It has three tables with a very welcoming underground space for small groups.

c/ Agullers, 7
Tel: 902 327 777

Ca l'Esteve
El Xampanyet

Before the building was built in 1868, wine was already served in the stables of the old palace that occupied the site where this emblematic spot stands today. Although in its beginnings it housed a bodega, it later began to serve tapas and small portions to workers and travellers who frequented the neighbouring El Born market. Situated in Carrer Montcada, very close to the Picasso Museum, this historic establishment, run by the third generation of the Ninou family, it maintains all the flavour of a bygone era and features in all the city tourist guides, which means it is continually packed with visitors who want to try its specialities, among which should be mentioned the anchovies, Iberian ham, Zamora cheese, baked vegetables on flat bread, *coca*, or the delicious seafood preserves. All of this, naturally, is accompanied by a glass of *xampanyet*, the popular sparkling wine the fame of which has ended up giving its name to the establishment.

c/ Montcada, 22
Tel: 93 319 70 03

01_kidney beans with streaky bacon and *botifarra* sausage
02_cuban rice
03_barcelona rice
04_cod rice
05_parellada rice
06_cod fritters
07_cannelloni a la *barcelonesa*
08_*empedrat* salted cod with white beans
09_russian salad
10_*escalivada* baked vegetables
11_*escudella barrejada* mixed broth
12_*escudella i carn d'olla* broth with stewed meat
13_spinach with raisins and pine nuts
14_*esqueixada* cod salad
15_casseroled noodles
16_chick peas with cod and spinach
17_sautéed peas and broad beans
18_broad beans *a la catalana*
19_tomatoes of montserrat with anchovies
20_fat thursday omelette
21_*xató* almond and hazelnut sauce

recipes
for starters

01_ mongetes amb cansalada i botifarra esparrecada

kidney beans with streaky bacon and *botifarra* sausage

for 4 people

* 600 g of cooked kidney beans * 4 slices of streaky bacon * 3 *botifarres del perol* * 2 cloves of garlic * 1 bunch of parsley * 4 spoonfuls of olive oil * pepper * salt

1. Peel and chop the cloves of garlic. Wash the parsley, dry it with absorbent paper and chop it. Make a long cut in the botifarras and chop them up so that they crumble completely on frying them.

2. Heat a spoonful of oil in a pan and brown the slices of streaky bacon on both sides until they get the colour. Remove them and, in the same oil, sauté the botifarres until they have completely crumbled and begin to brown.

3. Add the rest of the oil and chopped garlic. Cook one minute more and add the kidney beans. Season and cook for 4 minutes. Sprinkle them with parsley and serve them nice and hot together with the slices of streaky bacon.

The *botifarra del perol* is a speciality that is usually used crumbled up (*esparrecada*) and sautéed together with pulses, spinach, mushrooms...

To prepare this dish, kidney beans *del ganxet* are ideal, also called *montmelones*–, flat, kidney-shaped and very creamy, very popular in the counties of Vallès.

02_ arròs a la cubana
cuban rice

for 4 people

* 4 eggs * 4 cups of rice * 6 ripe tomatoes * 2 onions * 1 green pepper * 1 laurel leaf * 2 cloves of garlic * 1 bunch of parsley * 4 bananas * olive oil * pepper * salt

1. Boil a large amount of salted water in a saucepan with the laurel leaf. Pour in the rice and cook on a medium flame for 16 minutes. Drain and put to one side.

2. Peel and chop the onions and the clove of garlic. Wash the parsley, dry it with absorbent paper and chop it finely. Wash the pepper, dry it and cut it into strips. Make a crossway cut in the base of the tomatoes and scald them for 1 minute in saucepan with boiling water. Peel them, remove the seeds and chop them.

3. Sauté the onion on a low flame for 8 minutes in a frying pan with four spoonfuls of oil. Add the chopped garlic and the strips of pepper and cook for 2 more minutes. Add the chopped tomato and the chopped parsley, Season and leave to cook for 10 minutes until obtaining a sauce base.

4. Cut the bananas in half longitudinally and fry them in a frying pan with lots of hot oil for 1 minute. Fry the eggs.

5. Put the rice on the plates, cover them with some spoonfuls of sauce and accompany with the bananas and the fried eggs.

This popular recipe reached Barcelona with the Catalan *americanos*, who made their fortunes in Cuba. In its original version it was served with the inevitable frijoles and in Cuba, of course, the bananas used were green plantains or *machos*.

03_ arròs barcelonès
barcelona rice

for 4 people

* 4 cups of rice * 200 g of clams 200 g of cuttlefish * 150 g of squid * 8 prawns * 2 onions * 3 ripe tomatoes * 1 clove of garlic * 30 g of ham cubes * 50 g of *sobrassada* * olive oil * salt

1. Make a crossway cut in the base of the tomatoes and scald them in a saucepan of boiling water for 2 minutes. Drain them, peel them, remove the seeds and chop them.

2. Peel and chop the onions and the clove of garlic. Chop the cuttlefish and squid.

3. Heat four spoonfuls of oil in a pan and sauté the cuttlefish and squid for 4 minutes. Add the chopped onion and cook on a low flame for 8 more minutes. Add the chopped garlic, cook for one minute and add the tomato, the cubes of ham and the *sobrassada*. Season and leave to cook on a low flame for 10 minutes.

4. Add the rice, stir and cover with double the quantity of water or stock. Leave to cook on a medium flame for 17 minutes. Half way through, add the clams and prawns.

This recipe is an adaptation of the *Arroz barcelonés* from the recipe book *Carmencita o la buena cocinera*, the first edition of which was published in Barcelona in 1895. As the cuisine historian Núria Bàguena documents in her book *Cuinar i menjar a Barcelona: 1850-1900* (2007), this popular manual was written by Doña Eladia M., widow of Carpinell, and has almost certainly been the cookbook most used by Catalan housewives for more than a century. Today it is still being republished.

04_ arròs de bacallà
cod rice

for 4 people

* 4 cups of rice * 8 cups of water or broth * 400 g of desalted cod in pieces * ½ cauliflower * 50 g of peas * 2 artichokes * 1 green pepper * 1 onion * 3 ripe tomatoes * 2 cloves of garlic * 20 g of almonds * 6 threads of saffron * olive oil * pepper * salt

1. Peel the onion and the cloves of garlic. Clean the artichokes and cut them into six pieces. Grate the tomatoes. Wash the cauliflower and cut it into branches discarding the trunk. Wash the pepper and cut into squares.

2. Heat 1 dl of oil in a frying pan or saucepan and sauté the chopped onion until it is transparent. Add the artichokes, the green pepper and half the garlic and cook for 4 more minutes. Add the grated tomato, season and leave to cook for 8 minutes until obtaining a sauce.

3. Add the rice, sauté 1 minute and add the cod, the cauliflower branches and the peas. Season again and leave to cook on a medium flame for 18 minutes.

4. Prepare a sauce base crushing the roasted almonds with half the garlic and the threads of saffron. Dilute it with a little stock and add it to the rice when there are 5 minutes left for cooking. Serve nice and hot.

It is preferable to add a little salt and rectify half way through cooking, depending on the saltiness of the cod.
Picades are used a lot in Catalan cuisine. They are added at the end of the cooking to give flavour and thicken stews and sauces. They can be made with almonds, hazelnuts, toasted bread, chicken, rabbit or monkfish liver, garlic, parsley...

05_ arròs Parellada
Parellada rice

for 4 people

* 4 cups of rice * 8 cups of water or stock * 300 g of chicken * 100 g of pork loin * 4 sausages
* 8 mussels * 4 prawns * 100 g of cuttlefish * 100 g of monkfish * 25 g of peas * 2 artichokes
* 3 ripe tomatoes * 1 onion * 2 cloves of garlic * 8 threads of saffron * olive oil * pepper * salt

1. Cut the chicken, pork and sausages into pieces. Peel the prawns and cut them into pieces. Cut the monkfish and cuttlefish into cubes. Open the mussels by steam and remove the valves. Peel and chop the onion and the cloves of garlic. Grate the tomato. Clean the artichokes and cut each one into six pieces.

2. Heat 1 dl of oil in a frying pan and brown the chicken and the sausages for 4 minutes. Add the cubes of pork loin and cook 2 more minutes. Remove the meats, season them and put to one side. In the same oil sauté the cubes of cuttlefish for 2 minutes. Add the prawns and the monkfish and cook for 2 more minutes. Remove them and put to one side.

3. Cook the onion for 6 minutes. Add the chopped garlic and the artichokes and cook 2 more minutes. Add the grated tomato, Season and cook on a low flame for 8 minutes, until obtaining a good sauce base.

4. Add the rice, sauté it for 1 minute and add the meats and fish. Cover with a hot stock, add the peas and the saffron and cook for 18 minutes. Serve immediately.

This dish is attributed to the Barcelona dandy Juli Parellada, a regular client of the historic and now-disappeared Café-Restaurante El Suizo at the end of the 19th century. It is also known as *arròs sense entrebancs* (rice without nuisances), *arròs a la mandra* (lazy rice) or *arròs a la gandula* (layabout rice).

06_ bunyols de bacallà
cod fritters

for 6 people

* 300 g of desalted cod * 200 g of flour * 75 g of butter * 3 eggs * 3 cloves of garlic * 1 bunch of parsley * olive oil * pepper * salt

1. Place the cod in a saucepan of water and heat it. Just as it starts boiling, remove the saucepan from the flame, drain the cod and crumble it. Put to one side 2 dl of the stock obtained.

2. Crush the cloves of garlic con the chopped parsley in the mortar. Mix with the crumbled cod and put to one side.

3. Heat 2 dl of the cod stock with the butter in a saucepan. When it boils, add the flour in one movement and stir until the mass that is formed comes unstuck from the sides. Remove the saucepan from the stove and gradually add the beaten eggs one by one, stirring well before adding the next one.

4. Mix the mass obtained with the crushed ingredients from the mortar and season lightly. Make balls of the mass with a teaspoon and fry them in groups in a frying pan with abundant hot oil until they are browned. Serve the fritter immediately.

The secret of choux pastry is in the amount of beaten egg. It is a good idea to add the third egg gradually and check the tip of the dough. It will be perfect when it forms a "duck's beak" that does not come unstuck from the wooden spatula. The dough can be enriched with boiled potato.

07_ canelons a la barcelonesa
cannelloni a la barcelonesa

for 4 people

✳ 12 squares of cannelloni ✳ 150 g of beef ✳ 150 g of lean pork ✳ 100 g of chicken breast ✳ 1 chicken liver ✳ 50 g of lamb's brain ✳ 2 onions ✳ 1 tomato ✳ a pinch of thyme ✳ ½ teaspoonful of nutmeg ✳ 1/2 glass rancio wine or sherry ✳ 2 spoonful of brandy ✳ 2 slices of bread ✳ 50 g of grated cheese ✳ 2 cloves of garlic ✳ olive oil ✳ butter ✳ pepper ✳ salt

<u>For the béchamel</u>: ✳ 500 ml of milk ✳ 40 g of butter ✳ 40 g of flour ✳ a pinch of nutmeg ✳ pepper ✳ salt

1. Peel and chop the onions and the garlic. Chop up all the meats. Grate the tomato. Leave the inside part of the bread and soak with milk.

2. Heat the flour in a frying pan, add the butter and milk and cook on a low flame stirring continuously with a whisker until it thickens. Season and add a pinch of nutmeg.

3. Brown all the meats in a saucepan and cook for 30 minutes. Half way through add the onion and the chopped garlic. Pour in the rancio wine and brandy and cook 2 more minutes. Add the brains, the liver and the grated tomato and cook 10 more minutes. Debone the meats and chop all of it. Mix with the drained breadcrumb.

4. Cook the cannelloni in abundant salted water. Drain them and spread them over a clean tea towel. Spread the filling, roll up the cannelloni and place them on an oven tray. Cover them with the béchamel and sprinkle the grated cheese and some knobs of butter. Grate in the oven at 200° C until they brown. Serve immediately.

Cannelloni is a typical dish of the annual festival. They are very popular on Boxing Day to make use of the leftovers of the Christmas Day *escudella i carn d'olla* stew and meat.

empedrat salted cod with white beans

for 4 people

* 500 g of cooked white beans * 300 g of desalted cod * 2 spring onions * 1 Montserrat tomato
* 1 green pepper * 1/2 red pepper * 3 spoonfuls of black olives from Aragon * 5 spoonfuls of
extra virgin olive oil * 2 spoonfuls of Jerez vinegar * pepper * salt

1. Wash the tomato, dry it and cut it in squares. Wash the peppers, dry them, deseed them and cut them into squares of the same size. Peel and chop the spring onions. Drain and crumble the cod.
2. Prepare a vinaigrette beating the vinegar with the salt and pepper. Add the oil in a thread and continue beating until obtaining an emulsified sauce.
3. Place the beans in a salad bowl and cover them with the crumbled cod, the tomato, the spring onion and the peppers. Sprinkle with black olives and season with the vinaigrette. Put to one side in the fridge until serving.

To complete this nutritional salad you can add some hard-boiled eggs cut in two.

There are many versions of this popular kidney bean salad. Here we present a version related to the cod *esqueixada*. As the gastronome Manuel Vázquez Montalbán very poetically stated, "...an *empedrat* is never the same as another possible *empedrat*, as if it were a cursed, lost gastronomic concept...".

09_ ensaladilla russa
russian salad

for 4 people

* 150 g of tuna in oil * 3 potatoes * 2 eggs * 100 g of peas * 100 g or haricot green beans * 50 g of olives stuffed with anchovy * 2 carrots * 30 cl of mayonnaise * salt

1. Cook the eggs in boiling water for 10 minutes. Drain them, leave them to cool, peel and chop them. Wash, trim and chop the green beans.

2. Peel the potatoes and cut them into cubes. Peel the carrots and cut them into small cubes the same size as the potatoes. Cook the cubes of potato and carrot in salted boiling water for 10 minutes. They must be cooked but whole. Half way through, add the peas and the green beans. Drain and leave to cool.

3. In a salad bowl mix all the vegetables with the olives, hard-boiled egg and crumbled tuna. Add the mayonnaise, stir and serve.

This cold salad was created in the Hermitage restaurant from Moscow in the mid-19th century. In Russia it is known as "Olivier Salad" in honour of its creator, the chef Lucien Olivier. In Spain it became an essential recipe in both private homes and in tapas bars.

10_

escalivada
mixed baked vegetables

for 4 people

* 3 red peppers * 2 aubergines * 2 onions * 4 spoonfuls of olive oil * 1 spoonful of Jerez vinegar
* salt

1. Pre-heat the oven to 200°C. Wash the aubergines and the peppers and place them on a baking tray along with the onions without the skin.

2. Bake the vegetables. Calculate around 55 minutes for the peppers, 1 hour 10 minutes for the aubergines and 1 hour 30 minutes for the onions.

3. Once baked, wrap the peppers and aubergines in silver paper or a clean tea towel and leave them to cool. Then peel them and cut them into strips. Peel the onion and cut it in laminas.

4. Place the baked vegetables on a dish so that they are decoratively distributed by colour. Season them with a pinch of salt and dress with olive oil and vinegar.

Escalivar means "roasting on the embers of the barbecue". This dish is delicious as the vegetables are roasted on char-coal embers.
The peppers and aubergines are usually wrapped on removing them from the oven so that they are easier to peel.
This dish can be accompanied with some anchovies in oil, some herrings or some strips of cod.

escudella barrejada
mixed broth

for 8 people

* 125 g of rice * 125 g of noodles * 100 g of kidney beans * 2 onions * 2 potatoes * 1 carrot
* 4 cabbage leaves * 150 g pork rib * 1 ham bone * 4 pork backbones * 3 litres of water * salt

1. Leave the kidney beans to soak overnight. Peel the carrots and the potatoes. Wash the cabbage leaves.

2. Boil 4 litres of water with the kidney beans and all the meats. Bring to the boil and cook on a medium flame for 1 hour 30 minutes, removing the foam that forms on the surface.

3. Add all the vegetables and cook for 30 more minutes. Rectify with salt and pepper and add the noodles and the rice. Cook for 20 more minutes, leave to rest for 5 minutes and serve.

The *escudella barrejada* is a nutritional soup enriched with pasta, rice and, generally, a pulse such as chickpeas or kidney beans. There are many versions of this recipe, some of which include pumpkin, Swiss chard, spinach or even chestnuts, depending on the season.

12_

escudella i carn d'olla
broth with stewed meats

for 8 people

* 500 g of soup pasta, geletti or fusilli * 1 split pig's trotter, 1 pig's ear and 1 piece of beef snout
* 500 g of blood sausage * 1 piece of ham bone * 500 g of beef bones (knuckle or backbone)
* 1/2 chicken * 200 g of chickpeas * 1/2 cabbage * 4 potatoes * 2 sticks of celery * 2 carrots
* 2 parsnips * 2 onions * 1 leek * salt

For the *pilotes* (meatballs): * 200 g of lean minced pork * 100 g of beef * 2 cloves of garlic
* 1 bunch of parsley * a pinch of powdered cinnamon * 2 eggs * 6 spoonfuls of breadcrumbs
* flour

1. Leave the chickpeas to soak overnight. Wash and chop the cabbage. Peel the potatoes, onions, parsnips, carrot, leek and celery stick.

2. Place 6 litres of water in a saucepan with the chickpeas, bones, pig's trotter, ear and snout. Bring to the boil and cook for 30 minutes removing the foam that is formed on the surface. Add the chicken, cabbage, celery, parsnips and leek. Cook for 1 hour 30 minutes more.

3. Mix the chopped meats with the clove of garlic, slightly dampened and drained breadcrumbs, beaten eggs and finely chopped parsley. Season with salt, pepper and a pinch of cinnamon. Shape lengthened meatballs of about 12 cm long and 6 cm. Flour them and put to one side.

4. Add the pilotes and the potatoes to the saucepan and cook 30 minutes on a low flame. Add the blood sausage, season the stock and cook for 10 more minutes.

5. Strain 3/4 of the stock, keeping all the meat and vegetables in the first saucepan with the remaining hot stock. Bring the strained stock to the boil and add the pasta. Cook for some 15 minutes and serve.

The soup with pasta is generally served as a starter and the meat, vegetables, *botifarra* and *pilotes,* meatballs, as a second course.

13_ espinacs amb panses i pinyons
spinach
with raisins and pine nuts

for 4 people

* 1.5 kg of fresh spinach * 4 spoonfuls of Corinthian raisins * 3 spoonfuls of pine nuts
* 4 spoonfuls of oil * pepper * salt

1. Clean the spinach under the tap removing the roots from the base. Cook them for 4 minutes in a saucepan with 1 dl of water. Drain them in a sieve pressing with the back of a wooden spoon to remove the maximum amount of water. Put to one side.

2. Leave the raisins soaking in warm water for 30 minutes. Brown the pine nuts for 2 minutes in a non-stick frying pan with a few drops of olive oil.

3. Add the spinach and drained raisins, season lightly and cook together for 2 minutes, stirring often. Serve immediately.

This dish is also known as "Spinach a la catalana"
The raisins can be macerated in tea or white wine to give them more flavour.
You should be very careful because the pine nuts burn very quickly and become bitter. To avoid this, it is advisable to soak them for a few minutes before sautéing them.

esqueixada cod salad

for 4 people

* 500 g of cod loin * 2 ripe grated tomatoes * 1 small onion * 1 green pepper * 4 spoonfuls of black olives * 4 spoonfuls of extra virgin olive oil * pepper

1. Crumble the cod with your fingers into small strips under the tap.
2. Leave to soak, changing the water several times, for 4 hours. Peel the onion and cut it into rings. Grate the tomatoes.
3. Drain the cod and press it with your hands so that all the water is removed. Place the cod on a serving dish and mix it with the grated tomato, the onion rings and the black olives. Put to one side in the fridge for 1 hour and serve cold.

The verb *esqueixar* means "to strip off, to shred".
According to some people, this operation must always be done with the fingers and never using a knife.
In many versions this dish is completed with cubes of red or green pepper.

15_ fideus a la cassola
casseroled noodles

for 4 people
* 350 g of noodles * 8 sausages * 200 g of pork rib in pieces * 4 slices of blood sausage
* 2 tomatoes * 2 onions * 2 artichokes * 1 green pepper * 2 cloves of garlic * 1 bunch of parsley
* 1 laurel leaf * 1 glass of rancio wine or sherry * olive oil * pepper * salt

1. Peel and chop the onions and the cloves of garlic. Grate the tomatoes. Clean the pepper and cut it in squares. Clean the artichokes and cut them into eight pieces. Wash the parsley and chop it finely.

2. Heat three spoonfuls of oil in a saucepan and brown the sausages and pork rib on all sides for 4 minutes. Remove and put to one side.

3. Break up the blood sausage and cook it in the saucepan for 4 minutes. Put to one side.

4. Add four spoonfuls of oil to the saucepan and sauté the onion on a low flame for 8 minutes. Add half of the chopped garlic and the green pepper and cook 1 more minute. Add the grated tomato and cook for 8 more minutes. Season, pour in the rancio wine and increase the intensity of the flame. Leave to evaporate for 2 minutes.

5. Add all the meats kept aside and the artichokes, cover with water or stock and leave to cook for 5 more minutes. Rectify with salt, Add the noodles and cook them for the time shown by the maker. They should be soggy

6. Chop the remaining garlic with the parsley and add this mixture to the noodles when there is 2 minutes left for cooking. Serve the noodles immediately and hot.

Many versions of this recipe include a fistful of cooked kidney beans. The version prepared with cod tripe is particularly original.
This dish can also be served with an *allioli* sauce.

16_ cigrons amb bacallà i espinacs
chick peas
with cod and spinach

for 4 people

* 300 g of cooked chickpeas * 2 pieces of desalted cod * 1 bunch of spinach * 1 tomato
* 1 onion * 1 laurel leaf * 1 spoonful of chopped hazelnuts * 1 cup of stock * 2 cloves of garlic
* 1 bunch of parsley * 2 spoonfuls of flour for coating * a pinch of paprika * olive oil * pepper
* salt

1. Cut the cod into small cubes and lightly coat them in flour. Peel and chop the onion and the clove of garlic. Wash the parsley, dry it and chop it finely.

2. Heat three spoonfuls of oil on an earthenware casserole and brown the cubes of floured cod. Remove them and, in the same oil, sauté the chopped onion for 5 minutes on a very low flame. Add the chopped garlic and cook 1 more minute.

3. Add the chopped tomato and leave to cook on a very low flame for 4 minutes. Add the chickpeas, laurel leaf and season. Season with the paprika, pour in the stock and cook for 4 more minutes.

4. Add the cubes of cod and the spinach, cover and leave to cook all together for 10 more minutes. At the very end, sprinkle with the parsley and the chopped hazelnuts. Serve hot.

The stock should thicken slightly as if it were a sauce. It can also be prepared with shredded cod and served as a Lent stew. If it is prepared with four whole pieces of cod and loin it can be served as a second course or main dish, accompanied by some hard-boiled eggs.

17_ pèsols i faves ofegats
sautéed
peas and broad beans

for 4 people

* 750 g of peas * 1 kg of broad beans * 150 g of streaky bacon * 2 spring onions * 3 young garlics
* 1 glass of white wine * 1 branch of mint * 1 teaspoonful of sugar * olive oil * salt

1. Peel the broad beans and the peas. Chop finely two or three leaves of mint. Cut the streaky bacon into strips. Peel and chop the onions and the young garlics.

2. Brown the strips of bacon in an earthenware casserole with two spoonfuls of oil. As soon as they brown, add the chopped onion. Continue cooking on a low flame for 7 minutes. Add the young garlics and cook 2 more minutes.

3. Season the sauce base, add the white wine and raise the intensity of the flame. Let the wine reduce for 2 minutes and add the peeled peas and broad beans. Cover with water, rectify with salt and season with the teaspoonful of sugar and chopped mint.

4. Cover the casserole and leave to cook on a low flame for 30 minutes, stirring two or three times for cooking. Decorate with a leaf of mint and serve hot.

This dish is typical of Sant Andreu de Llavaneres and all the Maresme, the county of the "golden peas". It is prepared with the *garrofal*, *floreta* and *ganxo* varieties.

The dish can be completed with hard-boiled eggs or some slices of blood sausage that are added to the stew at the end of the cooking time.

18_ faves a la catalana
broad beans a la catalana

for 4 people

* 500 g of peeled broad beans * 200 g of streaky bacon * 3 spring onions * 2 young garlics
* 250 g of blood sausage * 1 teaspoonful of Pernod or aniseed spirit * 1 bunch of fresh mint
* 1 laurel leaf * a pinch of sugar * olive oil

1. Peel and chop the spring onions and young garlics. Cut the bacon into cubes and the blood pudding into thick slices. Fry the bacon and once fried put it in the casserole where the broad beans will be cooked.

2. Heat four spoonfuls of oil in a saucepan and sauté the chopped onion on a low flame for 8 minutes. Add the young garlics and cook 2 more minutes.

3. Add the broad beans, sugar, laurel leaf and the bunch of mint. Season, pour in the spirit and add a cup of water, just enough to cover the broad beans.

4. Cover the saucepan and leave to cook on a very low flame for about 20 minutes. Half way through, add the slices of blood sausage. Serve immediately.

The writer and gastronome Manuel Vázquez Montalbán considered this dish as one of the pillars of Catalan cuisine in "unmistakeable hegemony with the supreme triad" that completed the *escudella* and the *botifarra amb mongetes* (*botifarra* sausage with kidney beans)".

You can add rancio wine, thyme and a little grated tomato. The blood sausage is crumbled with the cooking; in some recipes a part is left crumbled and the kidney beans are cooked with another whole *botifarra* without cutting that is later served in slices.

19_ tomàquets de Montserrat amb anxoves
Montserrat tomatoes
with anchovies

for 4 people

* 4 Montserrat tomatoes * 16 salted anchovies * 3 spoonfuls of black olives from Aragon
* 1 spoonful of capers * 4 spoonfuls of olive oil * 1 spoonful of Jerez vinegar * pepper * salt

1. Clean the anchovies under the tap removing all the salt, the backbone and side bones. Cover the cleaned fillets with olive oil, some drops of vinegar and a pinch of pepper and leave them to macerate for at least one hour.

2. Wash the tomatoes, cut them into thick slices and arrange them on a service dish.

3. When serving, season the tomatoes with a pinch of salt and dress them with abundant olive oil and a thread of vinegar. Place the fillets of anchovy on top and add the black olives and capers. Serve immediately.

The variety known as "Montserrat tomato" has a colouring between green and pink, which is why it is also called the "pink tomato". It has some very characteristic protuberances and is hollow inside. They are very tasty and aromatic.

20_ truita de dijous gras
fat thursday omelette

for 4 people

* 4 eggs * 1/2 egg *botifarra* * some drops of olive oil * salt

1. Cut the *botifarra* into fine slices. Heat up some drops of oil in a frying pan and sauté them on a low flame a few at a time for one minute.

2. Beat the eggs with a pinch of salt and add the slices of egg *botifarra*.

3. Set the omelette on both sides and serve immediately.

Pork cuisine has always taken a leading role during the days of Carnival, before the privations of Lent.
It is traditional to eat these omelettes on Fat Thursday as an afternoon snack. The Baron of Maldà spoke of *botifarra* omelettes in a text as long ago as 1771.

21_

xató almond and hazelnut sauce

for 4 people

* 1 curly endive * 150 g of desalted cod * 8 fillets of anchovy in oil * 1 small tin of tuna in oil
* 4 spoonfuls of arbequina olives

<u>For the *xató* sauce</u>: * 20 g or roasted hazelnuts * 10 g of roasted almonds * 3 *nyora* peppers
* 4 slices of bread * 2 cloves of garlic * 1 cup of olive oil * 8 spoonfuls of vinegar * salt

1. Remove the stem and interior seeds of the *nyora* peppers and scald them in a saucepan with boiling water. Remove the pulp stuck to the skin with the point of a knife. Wet the inside part of the bread with vinegar.

2. In the bowl of the mixer or a mortar crush the almonds, hazelnuts, drained bread, cloves of garlic, pulp of the *nyora* peppers and olive oil. Season with a pinch of salt and blend until obtaining a reddish sauce.

3. Wash the escarole and break it up with your fingers. Tear the cod into strips and spread them over the salad together with the tuna and the anchovies.

4. Dress the salad with the *xató* sauce, sprinkle the olives on top and serve immediately.

The *xató* sauce has its origin in El Garraf and El Penedès.
The towns of Sitges, Vilanova i la Geltrú and El Vendrell argue about its authorship.
Escarole salad dresses with *xató* sauce is a typical winter dish. It is usually accompanied by varied omelettes: of green beans, white *botifarra*, artichokes or spinach.

01_hake meatballs
02_cod *a la llauna* in the pan
03_cod *a la manresana*
04_cod with honey
05_calamari filled with chocolate sauce
06_gaudí red mullets of ferran adrià
07_baby cuttlefish *a la barcelonesa*
08_sarsuela
09_*cap i pota* with *samfaina* head and leg
　　of beef with ratatouille
10_rabbit with chocolate
11_*fricandó* fricassee
12_pork loin kidney beans
13_pigs trotters filled with wild mushrooms
　　and prawns
14_roast chicken with *samfaina* ratatouille
15_beef with wild mushrooms

Meat and fish recipes

01_ mandonguilles de lluç
hake meatballs

for 4 people

∗ 800 g of cleaned hake fillets ∗ 2 eggs ∗ 2 onions ∗ 3 tomatoes ∗ 3 cloves of garlic ∗ 300 g of peas ∗ 50 g of raisins ∗ 3 spoonfuls of breadcrumbs ∗ 1 laurel leaf ∗ a pinch of cinnamon ∗ 1 spoonful of toasted almonds ∗ 1 bunch of parsley ∗ olive oil ∗ pepper ∗ salt

1. Leave the raisins to soak. Cook the hake fillets in a saucepan with salted boiling water and laurel leaf for 5 minutes. Drain them well in a sieve and crumble them, making sure no skin and bones remain. Put the cooking stock to one side.

2. Mix the hake with the beaten eggs, season and add the breadcrumbs and finely chopped parsley.

3. Form meatballs with the mixture, coat in flour and fry them in groups in a frying pan with hot oil for 4 minutes. Drain them on kitchen paper and put them to one side.

4. Sauté the chopped onion in a saucepan on a very low flame for 12 minutes. Add two cloves of chopped garlic and cook 2 more minutes. Add the tomatoes, peeled and chopped, and cook 12 more minutes until obtaining a sauce. Add the peas, season and sprinkle on cinnamon.

5. Add the meatballs and raisins to the saucepan, cover with some spoonfuls of the reserved stock and leave to cook on a low flame for 10 minutes.

6. Prepare a sauce base crushing the almonds with the remaining clove of garlic and parsley, add to the stew and cook 2 more minutes. Sprinkle with chopped parsley and serve immediately.

A version of this recipe was provided by the Restaurateurs Guild of Barcelona to the gastronome Carme Casas for its publication in the book *Barcelona a la carta* (1981) as representative of the city's cuisine.

02_ bacallà a la llauna
cod *a la llauna* in the pan

for 4 people

* 700 g of desalted cod loins * 1 ripe tomato * 4 cloves of garlic * 1 glass of dry white wine
* 1 bunch of parsley * 2 teaspoonfuls of paprika *de la Vera* * flour * 1 dl of olive oil * pepper * salt

1. Peel and fillet the garlic cloves. Grate the tomato. Wash and chop the parsley. Pre-heat the oven at 200°C.

2. Coat the pieces of cod with flour and fry them for 1 minute on each side in a frying pan with hot oil. Drain them on kitchen paper, season them lightly and place them on a refractory tray.

3. Brown the garlic in the same oil until they start to take on the colour. Add the grated tomato, season and cook for 4 minutes. Add the paprika, cook for 1 more minute and pour on the white wine. Turn the flame up and cook for 2 minutes. After this time, pour the sauce over the pieces of cod.

4. Bake at 200°C for 8 minutes, sprinkle with the chopped parsley and serve immediately.

This simple dish is one of the most typical recipes of all Catalan cuisine. It first appeared in Barcelona's inns in the 18th century and owes its name to the *llauna* (tin) or metal tray in which the fish was baked.

Some recipes, instead of sauce, add only a fry mixture of paprika and garlic, soaked with white wine and thickened with breadcrumbs.

03_ bacallà a la manresana
cod *a la manresana*

for 4 people

* 4 pieces of cod loin * 1 bunch of young spinach * 35 g of raisins * 30 g of pine nuts * 75 g of prunes * flour for coating * olive oil

1. Lightly flour the pieces of cod and fry them in a frying pan with three spoonfuls of olive oil for 1 minute on each side. Put them to one side.

2. In another frying pan with a few drops of oil, lightly sauté the spinach until they soften a little (they should still be crispy).

3. Remove them from the pan, add two spoonfuls of oil and sauté the prunes and raisins for 2 minutes. Add the pine nuts and continue cooking for 1 more minute, taking care not to burn them.

4. Pour the prunes, raisins and pine nuts on top of the cod and serve immediately.

Two quite different specialities are known in Manresa with the same name. The second version is made by frying some pieces of previously flour-coated cod. It is later covered with an *allioli* sauce mixed with apple or quince purée and cooked au gratin for a few minutes in the oven before serving.

04_ bacallà amb mel
cod with honey

for 4 people

* 400 g of desalted cod fillet * 150 g of flour * 1.5 glasses of water * 1 spoonful of honey
* 1 teaspoonful of powdered yeast * olive oil * salt

For the salad with raisins and pine nuts: * some escarole leaves * 1 oak leaf lettuce * 2 spoonfuls
of raisins * 2 spoonfuls of pine nuts * 6 spoonfuls of olive oil * 2 spoonfuls of Módena balsam
vinegar * pepper * salt

1. Wash the salad, drain it, chop it and place it in the salad bowl. Leave the raisins to soak in warm water for 30 minutes. Toast the pine nuts in a non-stick frying pan with a thread of oil. Prepare the vinaigrette beating the oil with the vinegar, salt and pepper until obtaining an emulsion sauce.

2. Prepare the batter mixing the flour with water, yeast and honey until obtaining a smooth, uniform mass with the desired texture.

3. Cut the cod into strips, lightly flour them and pass them through the batter. Fry the cod in groups for 3 minutes in a frying pan with abundant hot oil. Drain it on kitchen paper and season with a pinch of salt.

4. Distribute the salad on the service plates, sprinkle with the drained raisins and toasted pine nuts and dress with the vinaigrette. Place the cod strips beside it and serve immediately.

Frying strips of cod must be done quickly. We should realise that, on containing honey, the batter immediately takes on colour.

It is a medieval recipe the origin of which could be in the monastery of Poblet.

05_ calamars farcits amb salsa de xocolata
calamari filled
with chocolate sauce

for 4 people

∗ 12 calamari ∗ 2 onions ∗ 2 tomatoes ∗ 1 carrot ∗ 2 cloves of garlic ∗ 1 laurel leaf ∗ 2 spoonfuls of brandy ∗ 10 g of chocolate ∗ 1 spoonful of chopped hazelnuts ∗ 1 bunch of parsley ∗ olive oil ∗ pepper ∗ salt

For the filling: ∗ 2 onions ∗ 1 courgette ∗ 1 green pepper ∗ 1 carrot ∗ 1 clove of garlic ∗ 6 slices of bread ∗ 1 glass of milk ∗ some leaves of mint ∗ pepper ∗ salt

1. Clean the calamari removing the insides, eyes, beak and cartilage. Chop the side fins and tentacles finely and leave the body sacks whole.

2. Filling: sauté the onions in a frying pan with three spoonfuls of oil. Add the chopped garlic, the chopped tentacles and fins and the courgette, carrot and green pepper in very small cubes. Cook on a low flame for 8 minutes. Add the breadcrumbs, soaked in milk and drained, and the chopped mint. Mix, season and put to one side.

3. Fill the calamari with this preparation and fix them with a toothpick. Brown them for 1 minute on each side in a non-stick frying pan with a thread of olive oil. Put to one side.

4. Sauté the onion in a saucepan until it is transparent. Add the chopped garlic and peeled and chopped tomato and cook for 12 minutes. Add the filled calamari and flambé with the brandy, cover and leave to cook altogether for 15 minutes.

5. Pass the sauce through a manual food mill. Prepare a sauce base with the hazelnuts and chocolate and add it to the sauce. Cook together for 5 more minutes and serve immediately.

Chocolate sweetens the acidity of the tomato sauce base. This recipe reflects the influence of Empordà cuisine. It can be prepared with chicken, rabbit, monkfish or lobster dishes.

06_ molls Gaudí de Ferran Adrià
Gaudí red mullets
of Ferran Adrià

for 4 people

* 4 red mullets of 50 g * 1 small red pepper * 1 small courgette * 1 shallot * 1 small ripe tomato * 2 spoonfuls of chopped spring onion

For the salad: * 2 shallots or 2 spring onions * 4 anchovy fillets * 1 teaspoonful of toasted pine nuts * 1 teaspoonful of Módena vinegar * 2 spoonfuls of extra virgin olive oil * 4 spoonfuls of red pepper vinaigrette

1. Clean los red mullets, separate the fillets and remove the bones with some pincers. Peel the tomato, deseed it and cut it into cubes. Peel and cut the rest of the vegetables into cubes of the same size and mix them with the chopped spring onion.

2. Lightly spread the red mullet fillets on the skin side with olive oil. Place the mosaic of vegetables on top as if it were a pie. Season.

3. Cut the shallots into very thin slices and dress them with a julienne of anchovy, pine nuts, oil and Módena vinegar.

4. Brown the fillets on the vegetable side in a non-stick frying pan for a few seconds. Turn them over and cook them for 10 more seconds. Place the red mullet fillets on each plate with a few drops of vinaigrette between them and serve them with the salad.

The vinaigrette of red peppers is prepared by beating some spoonfuls of roast red pepper purée with olive oil, Jerez vinegar, salt and pepper.

This dish, inspired by *trencadís*, –the broken ceramic mosaics created by Gaudí , appeared on the cover of the first recipe book by Ferran Adrià: *El Bulli; el sabor del Mediterráneo* (1993).

07_ sepiones farcides a la barcelonesa
baby cuttlefish
a la barcelonesa

for 4 people

* 4 small cuttlefish * 50 g of Parma ham in cubes * 200 g of minced pork * 8 skins of pig's liver * 2 cloves of garlic * 2 tomatoes * 1 onion * 200 g of cooked chickpeas * 1 cup of *allioli* sauce * 1 glass of white wine * 1 bunch of parsley * 1 egg + 1 egg yolk * olive oil * pepper * salt
<u>For the sauce base</u>: * 1 spoonful of peeled hazelnuts * 1 clove of garlic * 1 bunch of parsley

1. Chop finely the cubes of ham and mix them with the mincemeat, egg and one clove of chopped garlic. Add abundant parsley, season and mix. Crush the ingredients of the sauce base.

2. Clean the cuttlefish. Chop the fins and tentacles and sauté them in a frying pan with a thread of oil for 2 minutes. Add them to the mincemeat, mix and fill the cuttlefish. Wrap them in the pig liver skins and brown them for 2 minutes on each side in a frying pan with a few drops of oil. Season them and put to one side.

3. Sauté the chopped onion in a saucepan. Add the remaining chopped garlic and cook 2 more minutes. Add the tomatoes, peeled and chopped, and cook for 12 minutes. Season and put to one side.

4. Add the cuttlefish to the saucepan. Wet with the wine and cook on a strong flame for 1 minute. Cover with a little water, cover the pot and cook for 30 minutes.

5. Add the chickpeas, the sauce base and the egg yolk. Cook altogether for 5 more minutes and serve immediately with the *alioli* sauce apart.

Picades are used in Catalan cuisine to thicken sauces of stews, integrating their ingredients and giving them flavour. If you want, you can add to the *picada* the pulp of a *nyora* pepper or a chilli pepper, previously soaked.

sarsuela

for 4 people

∗ 400 g of monkfish in 4 pieces ∗ 400 g of dorado or sea bass in 4 pieces ∗ 4 prawns ∗ 4 Dublin Bay prawns ∗ 2 medium calamari cut in rings ∗ 16 mussels ∗ 16 clams ∗ 2 onions ∗ 3 tomatoes ∗ 2 cloves of garlic ∗ 1.5 dl of fish stock ∗ 1 glass of rancio wine of sherry ∗ 1 small glass of rum ∗ a pinch of cinnamon ∗ 1 laurel leaf ∗ flour ∗ olive oil ∗ pepper ∗ salt

1. Leave the clams to soak in salted water for 4 hours. Clean the mussels. Peel and chop the onions and the cloves of garlic. Grate the tomatoes. Coat the pieces of monkfish and dorado with flour.

2. Heat 1 dl of oil in a saucepan and sauté the fish for 2 minutes on each side. Remove them, season them and put them to one side. Sauté the Dublin Bay prawns and prawns in groups for 2 minutes, remove and season them.

3. In the same oil, sauté the onion for 8 minutes. Add the chopped garlic and cook 2 more minutes. Add the grated tomato, Season and cook on a very low flame for 8 more minutes.

4. Add all the fish and seafood to the saucepan except the calamari and clams. Pour in the rum and flambé. Add the rancio wine, laurel leaf and cinnamon. Turn up the flame and leave to reduce for a few moments. Cover with the hot stock. Add the calamari and clams. Leave to cook together for 5 more minutes and serve immediately.

You can add a splash of lemon juice for some extra flavour and some crushed fried bread to thicken.

This dish came from Barcelona at the end of the 19th century, in the middle of the Modernist period. Josep Pla was a big critic of the poor quality *sarsueles* that were imposed many years later on some of the restaurants of Barceloneta. However, Vázquez Montalbán always defended the argument that the end result of the dish depended on the quality of the fish and seafood used.

09_ cap i pota amb samfaina
cap i pota with *samfaina*
head and leg of beef with ratatouille

for 4 people

* 350 g of beef snout * 250 g beef trotters * 1 blood sausage * 2 aubergines * 1 courgette
* 3 tomatoes * 2 green peppers * 1 red pepper * 2 onions * 2 cloves of garlic * 1 bunch of parsley
* 1 laurel leaf * pepper * salt

1. Wash the snout and trotters and cook in a saucepan with abundant salted water and the laurel loaf. Cook on a low flame for 35 minutes. Then drain them, leave them to cool and chop them up.

2. Wash the aubergines, cut them into cubes, salt them and leave them to drain in a sieve for about 30 minutes so that all the bitter liquid is released. Then wash them under the tap and dry them.

3. Peel the onions and cut them into slices. Peel and chop the cloves of garlic. Wash the peppers and courgette and cut them into strips. Make a crossway cut in the base of the tomatoes and scald them for 1 minute in a saucepan with boiling water. Peel them, deseed them and cut them into strips.

4. Heat four spoonfuls of oil in a saucepan and sauté the onion on a low flame until it is transparent. Add the chopped garlic and the peppers and leave to cook for 5 more minutes. Add the tomato, the courgette and the aubergines and cook for another 10 minutes, stirring continuously. Then season, add a glass of water and leave to cook on a low flame for 25 more minutes.

5. Add the *cap-i-pota* to the *samfaina* and leave to cook altogether for 15 minutes. Add the blood sausage cut into slices and cook 5 more minutes. Sprinkle with chopped parsley and serve.

The *cap i pota* (head and leg, literally) is usually served accompanied by a sauce base or a *samfaina* (ratatouille), as in this recipe. If you want you can add a chilli and a teaspoonful of spicy paprika.

10_ conill amb xocolata
rabbit with chocolate

for 4 people

∗ 1 rabbit ∗ 1 carrot ∗ 1 leek ∗ 1 onion ∗ 2 glasses of red wine ∗ 1 small glass of brandy ∗ 50 g of chocolate fondant ∗ 1 clove of garlic ∗ 2 spoonfuls of pine nuts ∗ 2 spoonfuls of almonds ∗ 2 cups of stock ∗ 1 bunch of thyme ∗ 1 cinnamon stick ∗ 1 laurel leaf ∗ pepper ∗ salt

1. Peel the onion and the leek and cut them into small squares. Peel the carrot and cut it into small squares. Cut the rabbit into pieces, season it and leave it to macerate with the vegetables, wine, brandy, laurel, cinnamon and thyme for 12 hours.

2. Drain the pieces of macerated rabbit and brown them in groups for 4 minutes in a wide frying pan with 6 spoonfuls of oil. Place the pieces in an earthenware casserole.

3. In the same pan sauté the vegetables drained of the maceration liquid for 5 minutes on a very low flame. Add them to the casserole as well.

4. Add the maceration liquid to the pan with the aromatic herbs and leave to reduce on a high flame for 4 minutes. Add it to the casserole with the unpeeled clove of garlic and the stock.

5. Cover and cook altogether for 40 minutes on a very low flame. Then remove the pieces of rabbit, take out the clove of garlic and pass the sauce through a chinoise.

6. Toast the almonds and pine nuts in a frying pan and crush them with the clove of garlic and chocolate. Heat the rabbit with the sauce and sauce base for 4 more minutes and serve.

This dish can be completed with some sautéed prawns. It is a traditional recipe from the rich Empordà cuisine which, like so many others, has been popularly assimilated into the Barcelona cuisine.

11_ fricandó
fricassee

for 4 people

∗ 8 thin fillets of flank of beef ∗ 150 g of dried wild mushrooms ∗ 1 onion ∗ 3 tomatoes ∗ 1 cup of stock or water ∗ 1 glass of white wine ∗ 1 cup + 1 spoonful of flour ∗ 2 spoonfuls of olive oil ∗ 1 laurel leaf ∗ pepper ∗ salt

For the sauce base: ∗ 1 spoonful of toasted almonds ∗ 1 clove of garlic ∗ 1 spoonful de chopped parsley

1. Leave the mushrooms to soak in a bowl with warm water for 14 minutes. Season the fillets, coat them with flour and fry them in a saucepan with two spoonfuls of hot oil for 2 minutes on each side. Put to one side.

2. Peel the onion, chop it and sauté in the same saucepan for 8 minutes until it is transparent. Add the chopped tomatoes and leave to cook on a very low flame for 8 more minutes. Add a spoonful of flour, mix and cook for 2 more minutes.

3. Pour in the white wine and add the drained mushrooms and laurel. Leave to cook 5 more minutes and sprinkle with the stock. Season and cook on a low flame for 10 minutes. Add the meat and cook for 30 minutes on a very low flame.

4. Prepare a sauce base with a pestle and mortar crushing the toasted almonds with a clove of garlic and some parsley leaves. Add this base to the saucepan and leave to cook 10 more minutes so that the stew thickens before serving.

Fricassee is often made with dry fairy ring mushrooms (*moixernons*) but can be replaced by penny buns or any other type of dehydrated wild mushroom.

llom amb mongetes
pork loin kidney beans

for 4 people

⚘ 8 fillets of pork loin ✳ 400 g of cooked kidney beans ✳ 50 g of bacon or streaky bacon ✳ 2 spoonfuls of gravy ✳ 1 clove of garlic ✳ 1 bunch of parsley ✳ olive oil ✳ pepper ✳ salt

1. Fry the fillets of pork loin in a frying pan with two spoonfuls of oil until they brown a little. Remove them, season them and put to one side.

2. In the same frying pan brown the strips of bacon for 2 minutes. Add the chopped garlic, cook one more minute and add the cooked kidney beans.

3. Add the gravy, season and cook for 2 minutes. Sprinkle with the chopped parsley and serve immediately with the pork loin fillets.

This simple recipe is one of the identifying marks of Barcelona's cuisine. Just as Ignasi Domènech relates in his book *l a teca* (1924), this dish became popular in the 19th century in the Fonda del Falcó, where it was prepared inimitably. The secret was surely in the adding of a few spoonfuls of cooking stock from some roast meat to make it creamier and tastier.

13_ peus de porc farcits de bolets i gambes
pigs trotters filled with wild mushrooms and prawns

for 4 people

* 4 pigs trotters * 1 skin of pig liver * 450 g of assorted wild mushrooms * 16 prawn tails
* 4 onions * 2 carrots * 2 tomatoes * 3 cloves of garlic * 1 bunch of parsley * 1 bunch of thyme
* 1 glass of rancio wine or sherry * 2 spoonfuls of flour * olive oil * pepper * salt

To cook the pigs trotters: * 1 bunch of rosemary * 1 bunch of parsley * 2 cloves of garlic * 1 clove
* 1 onion * 1 carrot * a few grains of pepper * a pinch of salt

For the sauce base: * 1 clove of garlic * 2 spoonfuls of almonds * 2 biscuits of *carquinyolis*
* 1 bunch of parsley

1. Cook the trotters in a saucepan with abundant water and all the aromatic herbs for 3 hours. Drain them and debone them. Put the cooking stock to one side. Prepare a sauce base crushing all the ingredients in a mortar.

2. Sauté the mushrooms in a frying pan with two spoonfuls of oil, a chopped onion, a clove of chopped garlic and parsley for 7 minutes. Add the prawn tails and season. Cook 2 more minutes.

3. Fill the pig's trotters. Wrap them in the liver skin, coat in flour and brown them for 2 minutes on each side in a saucepan with three spoonfuls of olive oil.

4. In the same oil sauté the remaining chopped onions. Add the remaining garlic, carrots in small squares and the chopped en tomato. Add the wine, parsley and thyme. Season and cook for 10 minutes.

5. Add the filled pig's trotters to the saucepan and add some spoonfuls of cooking stock. Cover and cook altogether for 30 minutes. Add the sauce base to the stew, cook 5 more minutes and serve.

They can be filled with snails, blood sausage, shrimps... If you want, you can wrap them in cabbage leaves previously scalded in boiling water.

14_ pollastre rostit amb samfaina
roast chicken
with *samfaina* ratatouille

for 4 people

* 1 chicken * 2 red peppers * 1 aubergine * 1 green pepper * 1 onion * 3 tomatoes * 2 cloves of garlic * olive oil * pepper * salt

1. Cut the chicken into eight pieces and flambé them on the gas ring to eliminate any remains of feathers. Peel the onion and cut it into thin strips. Wash the peppers, dry them and cut them into square pieces. Wash the aubergine and cut it into cubes. Peel and chop the cloves of garlic.

2. Make a crossway cut in the base of the tomatoes. Scald them for 2 minutes in a saucepan with boiling water, Drain and peel them, deseed and chop them.

3. Heat three spoonfuls of oil in a saucepan and gently fry the pieces of chicken until they are browned. Remove them and, in the same oil, sauté the chopped onion for 5 minutes. Add the chopped garlic, cook for one more minute and add the chopped tomato. Cook for 5 minutes and add the chopped peppers and chicken. Season, add a small cup of water and cover.

4. Leave to cook on a very low flame for 50 minutes, adding a little more water if necessary. Half way through, add the aubergine cubes. Serve hot.

If this dish is prepared with El Prat chicken or another farmhouse chicken, you should calculate 25 minutes more cooking. The *samfaina* must be juicy and semi-liquid. Be careful that the stew does not dry up during cooking and add water or stock if necessary.

15_ vedella amb bolets
beef with wild mushrooms

for 4 people

* 1 kg of beef hock * 300 g of assorted wild mushrooms * 2 onions * 2 tomatoes * 2 carrots
* 2 medium size potatoes * 1 laurel leaf * 2 cloves of garlic * 2 cloves * 3 spoonfuls of rancio wine
or sherry * olive oil * pepper * salt

For the sauce base: * 1 spoonful of chopped hazelnuts * 2 spoonfuls of chopped almonds
* 1 clove of garlic * 1 bunch of parsley

1. Heat four spoonfuls of oil in a saucepan and brown the beef, cut into cubes, in two groups. Season them, put to one side and, in the same oil, sauté the chopped onions on a low flame for 8 minutes. Add the chopped garlic and cook 2 more minutes.

2. Add the peeled and chopped tomato and the carrots in slices. Soak with the wine. Turn up the flame and leave to reduce for 2 minutes. Then season and cook on a low flame for 5 more minutes.

3. Add the mushrooms, cloves and meat. Cover with water, cover and leave to cook on a very low flame for 1 hour. When there are still 20 minutes to complete the cooking, add the potatoes cut into small squares.

4. Prepare a sauce base in the mortar with the hazelnuts, almond, clove of garlic and parsley. Add this base to the stew when there are still 10 minutes left for cooking. Serve hot.

This recipe can also be prepared with rump steak or with other cuts of beef suitable for stewing.

barcelona_cuisine

01_swiss roll

02_lent fritters

03_pork scratching flat cake

04_saint john's flat cake

05_catalan custard

06_foams of Sitges

07_panellets catalan almond cookies
  with pine nuts

08_sweet potato pudding

09_cottage cheese with honey

recipes
for desserts

01_ braç de gitano
swiss roll

for 8 people
* 4 eggs * 75 g of sugar * 75 g of flour * 25 g of butter * 400 ml of whipping cream
* 50 g of icing sugar (2 spoonfuls)

1. Separate the whites from the yolks. Beat the yolks with the sugar with a whisker until they change colour. Add the sieved flour. Melt the butter, leave it to cool and add to the mixture.

2. Whip the whites into a meringue and add the previous mixture with encircling movements. Pre-heat the oven to 200°C.

3. Line an oven tray with baking paper and brush it lightly with butter. Pour on the mass and bake at 200°C for 7 minutes.

4. Remove the oven tray and remove the piece of cake from the tray with great care without removing the paper. While it is still hot, roll up the cake with the paper. When it is cold, unroll it again and remove the paper.

5. Whip the cream with the sugar. Extend the panel of cake and cover it with the whipped cream. Roll it up again and put to one side in the fridge for one hour.

6. When serving, have two spoonfuls of icing sugar ready in a sieve and sprinkle it giving light taps on the edge so that it covers the whole surface of the Swiss roll. Cut the ends to make the presentation uniform and serve.

In season you can mix the cream filling with some strawberries cut small.
For a more elegant presentation, heat a steel needle until it is red hot and caramelise the sugar on the surface forming diamonds.

02_ bunyols de quaresma
lent fritters

* 1 kg of flour * 6 eggs * 20 g of baking yeast * 250 g of sugar * 1 cup of oil * 1 glass of milk
* 3 spoonfuls of aniseed * 2 grated lemon rinds * 1 small glass of aniseed liquor * a pinch of salt
* oil for frying

1. Dissolve the yeast in the warm milk, add the grated lemon rind and mix with the flour. Gradually add the rest of the ingredients to obtain a uniform, smooth and elastic mass. Cover the mass with a tea towel and leave it to rest in a spot free of air currents for a minimum of 2 hours, until it has doubled in volume.

2. With your hand rubbed in oil, take portions of the mass and, if you want, shape them into rings. Fry the fritters in groups in a frying pan with very hot oil until they are golden.

3. Sprinkle them with sugar on removing them from the pan and leave them to drain on kitchen paper. Leave them to cool and serve.

There are many recipes for fritters, using more or less flour, according to the consistency and shape you want to give them.
It is a good idea to always have a cup of oil handy to rub on your fingers as the fritters are fried.

03_ coca de llardons
pork scratchings flat cake

for 6 people

* 1 sheet of puff pastry dough * 150 g of pork scratchings * 50 of sugar * 100 g of pine nuts
* 1 spoonful of aniseed * 1 egg yolk

1. Pre-heat the oven to 200°C. Chop up the pork scratchings with a mincer or kitchen blender.

2. Extend the sheet of puff pastry over a work surface and mark it widthways in three equal parts. Cover the central third with half of the pork scratchings and sprinkle with a third of the sugar. Cover with another third of the dough and pass over the roller.

3. Brush the surface with a little aniseed, add the remaining pork scratchings and sprinkle with another third of the sugar. Cover with the final third of the dough and flatten again with the roller.

4. Pinch the surface of the flat cake with a fork, brush it with the beaten egg yolk and sprinkle it with the pine nuts.

5. Bake at 200°C for 30 minutes. Leave to cool on a grille before serving.

This flat cake is the speciality of Carnival time and, very specifically, Fat Thursday. Today it is available throughout the year in cake shops and may also appear, along with other sweet flat cakes, on the eve of Saint John's Day.

04_ coca de sant joan
saint john's flat cake

for 8 people

✳ 300 g of flour ✳ 150 g of butter ✳ 3 eggs ✳ 40 g of sugar ✳ 15 g of baking yeast ✳ 2 spoonfuls of milk ✳ a pinch of salt

For the decoration: ✳ 100 g of glazed fruits ✳ 20 g of pine nuts ✳ 50 g of sugar ✳ 1 glass of muscatel ✳ 1 knob of butter

1. Cut all the glazed fruits and leave them to soak with the muscatel for 2 hours. Dissolve the yeast in a saucepan with the slightly warm milk. Add 225 g of flour, the sugar and a pinch of salt. Add the butter in bits, the beaten eggs and the remaining flour, stirring very slowly with the blender at minimum speed.

2. Mix well, cover with a tea towel and leave the dough to rest 4 hours so it can double in volume.

3. Grease and flour lightly the baking tray and place the extended dough on it in the shape of an oval flat cake. Spread the fruits and the pine nuts on top and sprinkle with sugar. Leave to rest in a spot free from air currents for 30 minutes. Pre-heat the oven to 180°C.

4. Bake the flat cake at 180°C for 30 minutes. Increase the temperature to 200°C and continue baking for 5 more minutes so that it is well browned. Leave to cool on a grille and serve.

It is said that in the past all the flat cakes on the eve of Saint John's Day were round as homage to the solar nature of the festival.

Traditional Catalan flat cakes are related to other similar preparations around the Mediterranean, both sweet and savoury.

05_ crema catalana
catalan custard

for 4 people

* 500 ml of milk * 4 egg yolks * 100 g + 12 spoonfuls of sugar * 20 g of starch or cornflour
* 1 small cinnamon stick * 1 piece of lemon peel

1. Bring the milk to boil together with the cinnamon and piece of lemon peel. As soon as it reaches boiling point, remove from the flame, cover and leave to cool.

2. Beat the egg yolks with 100 grams of sugar until they whiten. Add the starch and continue beating. Add some spoonfuls of warm milk and mix well until they are absorbed.

3. Mix the preparation of egg yolks with the rest of the milk, remove the lemon peel and place it on a very low flame again.

4. Cook for a few minutes without letting it boil and stir continuously until obtaining a creamy texture. Remove from the flame and pour it into a flat dish or in small individual earthenware casseroles.

5. Heat a special spatula for caramelising on the gas ring. Cover the custard with the remaining sugar and caramelise it at the last moment to obtain a crispy caramel layer.

This cream is the most typical dessert of Catalan cuisine and is inevitably associated with the festival of Saint Joseph. It is also known as "Saint Joseph's Cream".

All the milk and egg-based creams seem to have their origin in Occitan cuisine.

The diner is normally asked if they want the cream caramelised or if they want it without the crispy layer on top.

06_ escumes de Sitges
foams of Sitges

* 150 g of ground almonds * 50 g of flour * 200 g of icing sugar * 4 egg whites * 70 g of laminated almond * butter

1. Beat the whites to a merongue with a whisker. Add the sugar when the whites are half-whipped. Pre-heat the oven to 140°C.
2. Sieve the flour, mix it with the ground almond and add the merengue, mixing it with encircling movements, from top to bottom.
3. Using a piping bag or two spoons, form small heaps of about 2.5 cm on a baking tray lined with oven paper and slightly greased with butter.
4. Sprinkle the small merengue piles with laminated almond and sieve a little caster sugar over them. Bake at 140°C in the low part of the oven for 25 minutes or until they brown.

These traditional sweets, typical of the gastronomy of Sitges, are made with *marcona* almonds. They can also be aromatised with essence of lemon.
It is essential to accompany the tasting of the *escurnos* with a glass of Malvasia wine from Sitges, a sweet local wine made from the grapes of the same name.

07_ panellets de pinyons
panellets catalan almond cookies with pine nuts

* 500 g of ground almond * 500 g of sugar * 250 g of pine nuts * 2 eggs

1. Break the eggs and separate the yolks from the whites. Mix the ground almond with the sugar and the egg whites without kneading too much. If necessary, add a few drops of water. The dough must be humid yet crumbly. Pre-heat the oven to 220°C.

2. Make long cylinders of dough and place them on the work surface. Cut the cylinders into portions and roll them into balls with damp hands.

3. Mix the pine nuts with the beaten yolks and coat the marzipan balls with them, pressing lightly with damp palms so that they remain well stuck to the dough.

4. Line a baking tray with oven paper and place the panellets on it forming rows. Brush them, if you want, with more beaten egg yolk and bake them at 220°C for 10 minutes. Remove them from the oven and leave them to cool slightly before unsticking them from the tray to avoid them breaking.

Panellets are the typical sweets of All Saints Day all over Catalonia. They can be made in the most diverse forms, flavours and colours. The only secret consists of preparing a humid dough and avoid it drying during cooking. The pine nuts must be toasted but the inside must remain juicy and damp.

08_ púding de moniatos
sweet potato pudding

for 8 people

* 1 kg of sweet potatoes * 4 eggs * 50 g of butter * 100 ml of milk * 100 g of brown sugar
* a teaspoonful of cinnamon * 50 ml of muscatel

1. Wash the sweet potatoes and cook them without peeling in water for 40 minutes. Drain them, leave them to cool and chop them up.

2. Melt the butter in a frying pan or in the microwave oven. Pre-heat a bain-marie in the oven at 200°C.

3. Chop the sweet potatoes in the mixer until they become a purée. Add the eggs, sugar, melted butter and muscatel and continue mixing until obtaining a uniform mixture.

4. Grease a cake mould and pour in the prepared mass. Cook in the bain-marie at 200°C for 1 hour. Remove from the oven and leave to cool on a grille. Leave to rest for a minimum of 6 hours before removing from the mould so that it is well settled.

To give it an original touch you can add some raisins to the mass and replace the muscatel with a glass of aniseed liquor. This recipe, ideal for serving with *panellets* during the All Saints festival, appeared published in the historic cookbook *Carmencita o la buena cocinera* (1895) and was included by Núria Bàguena in her interesting study *Cuinar i menjar a Barcelona: 1850-1900* (2007).

09_ mel i mató
cottage cheese
with honey

for 4 people

* 300 g of cottage cheese * 6 spoonfuls of honey * a pinch of powdered cinnamon * 16 walnuts

1. Peel the nuts and chop them. Cut the cottage cheese into slices and place them on the dishes.

2. Slightly warm the honey in bain-marie or in the microwave oven so that it is a runny liquid.

3. Pour the honey in threads over the slices of cottage cheese. Sprinkle the chopped nuts and a pinch of powdered cinnamon. Serve immediately.

In Barcelona it was a big tradition to buy the cottage cheese made by the nuns from the caretakers of the convents. The mató of Pedralbes had great renown, as did that made by the farm women from the town near to Montserrat.
This simple recipe, of medieval origin, can be served on some slices of brioche It can also be prepared in the form of mousse or ice cream.

gourmet addresses

Grocers, gourmet shops and delicatessens

Camarasa c/ Torras i Pujalt, 48-50.
T 93 211 23 42. www.camarasafruits.es

Can Ravell c/ Aragó, 313.
T 93 457 51 14. www.ravell.com

Casa Pepe c/ Balmes, 377.
T 93 417 11 76. www.casapepe.es

Colmado Quílez Rambla Catalunya,
63. T 93 215 23 56. www.lafuente.es

Da Giorgio Avda. Sarrià 67, Benet y
Mateu 48 y Santaló, 115. T 93 322 86
59. www.dagiorgio.es

Delishop c/Travessera de Gràcia, 141
T 93 238 99 45. www.delishop.es

La Castafiore Aribau, 58.
T 93 323 41 08.

Mas Gourmets c/ Gran de Gràcia, 93
T 93 237 93 39.
www.masgourmets.com

Mestres Torradors Casa Gispert
c/ Sombrerers 23. T 93 319 75 35.
www.casagispert.com

Origen 99,9% Passeig de Born, 4,
c/ Vidrieria, 6-8, c/ Ramón y Cajal, 12
T 93 213 60 31

Queviures Múrria c/ Roger de Llúria, 85
T 93 215 57 89. www.murria.cat

Semon c/ Ganduxer 31.
T 93 240 30 88. www.semon.es

Tutusaus c/ Francesc Pérez Cabrero, 5
Industria, 165. T 93 209 83 73.
www.tutusaus.com

Vila Viniteca c/ Agullers, 9.
T 902 327 777. www. vilaviniteca.es

Cod, fish and seafood

Fishop Paseo de Gràcia, 53.
T 93 487 72 08. www.grupofishop.com

Genaro Mercat de la Boqueria. Parada
734. T 93 302 12 42.
www.mariscosgenaro.com

La casa del bacallà c/ Comtal, 8.
T 93 301 65 39

Martínez Plaça Font, 1. T 93 221 81 22.

Masclans Mercat de Galvany,
parada 213 y Mercat de les Corts.
T 93 200 99 27.
www.masclansgalvany.com

Pairó Fish Mercat de l'Abaceria
Central, parada 408. T 93 213 85 46.

Meat, poultry, hams and cured meats

Andreu C/ Giralt el Pellisser, 24.
T 93 295 50 72.
www.andreuxarcuteria.com

Avinova Mercat de la Boqueria, puesto
703-707. T 93 301 30 71.

Bragulat Plaça de la Llibertat, 25.
T 93 237 59 79.

Casa Alfonso c/ Roger de Llúria, 6.
T 93 301 97 83. www.casaalfonso.com

David Carnissers Mercat de Santa
Caterina, parada 8-9. T 93 319 21 42.

La Botifarreria de Santa Maria
c/ Santa Maria, 4. T 93 319 91 23.
www.labotifarreria.com

Mas Gourmets c/ Amigó, 60.
T 93 209 42 12.
www.masgourmets.com

Margarit Mercat de Sarrià, parada
61-64. T 93 203 69 68.
www.xmargarit.com

Reserva Ibérica c/ Aragó, 242.
T 93 272 49 74. www.reservaiberica.com

Xarcuteria Hom c/ Provença, 79.
T 93 439 82 35. www.xarcuteriahom.com

Cheeses

L'Hereu c/ Comte Borrell, 30.
T 93 441 28 34.

Queviures Múrria c/ Roger de Llúria,
85. T 93 215 57 89. www.murria.cat

Totformatge Passeig del Born, 13.
T 93 319 53 75.

Tutusaus c/ Francesc Pérez Cabrero,
5; Indústria, 165. T 93 209 83 73.
www.tutusaus.com

Vila Viniteca c/ Agullers, 9.
T 93 310 19 56. www. vilaviniteca.es

Mushrooms

Potràs Mercat de la Boqueria. Parada
867 870. T 93 302 52 73.
www.boletspetras.com

Oil

Oro líquido c/ Palla, 8.
T 93 302 29 80. www.oroliquido.es

Bakeries

Baluard c/Baluard 38-40.
T 93 221 12 08.
www.baluardbarceloneta.com

BarcelonaReykjavik C/ Doctor Dou,
12, C/ Princesa, 53 i C/ Asturies, 20.
T 93 302 09 21.
www.barcelonareykjavik.com

Forn de pà Fortino c/ Travossera de
Gràcia, 145. T 93 237 38 73.
www.fornfortino.com

Turris. c/Aribau, 158. T 93 217 96 00.
www.turris.es

Cake shops, chocolate and sweets

Bubó. c/ Caputxes, 10.
T 93 268 72 24. www.bubo.es

Baixas. c/ Muntaner 331.
T 93 209 25 42. www.baixas.es

Cacao Sampaka. c/ Consell de
Cent, 292. T 93 272 08 33. www.
cacaosampaka.com

Canal. c/ Muntaner, 566; Calvet, 15.
T 93 417 10 53. www.canal.es

Caelum c/ de la Palla, 8.
T 93 302 69 93.
www.caelumbarcelona.com

Chocolate Factory c/ Amigó, 53.
T 93 209 54 26.
www.chocolatfactory.com

Chocolateria Fargas
c/ del Pi, 16; Pl. Cucurulla, 2.
www.xocolatesfargas.com

Enric Rovira c/ Av. Josep Tarradelles,
113. T 93 419 25 47.
www.enricrovira.com

Foix de Sarrià Pl. de Sarrià, 9.
T 93 203 07 14. www.foixdesarria.com

Hofmann c/ Flassaders, 44.
T 93 268 82 21. www.hofmann-bcn.com

Escribà La Rambla, 83; Gran Via 546.
T 93 301 60 27. www.escriba.es

Natcha Avda. de Sarrià, 45.
T 93 430 10 70. www.natcha.cat

Ochiai. c/ Comte d'Urgell, 110.
T 93 453 63 83.
www.ochiaipastisseria.com

Oriol Balaguer Plaça Sant Gregori
Taumaturg, 2. T 93 201 18 46.
www.oriolbalaguer.com

Papabubble c/ Ample, 28.
T 93 268 86 25. www.papabubble.com

Sacha. c/ Vallmajor, 31. T 93 201 32 22.
www.pasteleriasacha.com

Xocoa. c/ Princesa, 10; Roger
de Llúria, 87. T 93 487 24 99.
www.xocoa-bcn.com

Torrons (nougats)

Casa Colominas. c/ Cucurulla, 2;
Portaferrissa, 8; Quevedo, 9; Gran de
Gràcia, 57. T 93 317 46 81.
www.casacolomina.com

Orxateria-Torroneria Sirvent.
c/ Parlament 56. T 93 441 27 20.
www.turronessirvent.com

Planelles Donat. Avda. Portal de
l'Àngel, 25 y Cucurulla, 9.
T 93 317 34 39. www.planellesdonat.com

Wine merchants

El Celler de Gelida. c/ Vallespir, 65.
T 93 339 26 41. www.cellerdegolida.net

**El Club del Gourmet de El Corte
Inglés** Plaça Catalunya, 14.
T 93 306 38 00. www.elcorteingles.es

Lafuente c/ Aragó, 241-243 y Juan
Sebastián Bach, 20. T 93 215 02 21
www.lafuente.es

L'Hereu c/ Comte Borrell, 30.
T 93 441 20 04.

Vilaviniteca Agullers, 7. T 93 268 32
27. www.vilaviniteca.es

Vinus & Brindis
c/Torrent de l'Olla, 147.
www.vinusbrindis.com

Xampany c/València, 200.
T 93 453 93 38.

gourmet addresses

Tea and coffee

Bon Mercat c/Pons i Gallarza, 9.
c/ Baixada de Llibreteria, 1.
T 93 315 29 08.
Cafés El Magnífico c/ Argenteria, 64.
T 93 319 39 75.
www.cafeselmagnifico.com
Ingredients: Cafè Centro Comercial
Gran Vía 2. c/ Gran Via, 75.
T 93 576 35 16. www.ingredientscafe.es
Sans & Sans c/ Argenteria, 59
T 93 310 25 18
www.sansisansbarcelona.com
Tealosophy c/ Bonavista, 3.
T 93 415 49 06. www.tealosophy.com
The Tea Centre of Barcelona
c/ Travessera de Gràcia, 122.
T 93 218 40 78.

Tapas

Bodega Manolo c/ Torrent de les
Flors, 101. T 93 284 43 77.
Ca l'Esteve – El Xampanyet
c/ Montcada, 22. T 93 319 70 03
Cervecería Catalana c/Mallorca,
236. T 93 216 03 68.
Ciudad Condal Rambla Catalunya,
18. T 93 318 19 97.
Cervecería José Luis
Avda. Diagonal, 520. T 93 200 75 63.
www.joseluis.es
El Vaso de Oro c/ Balboa, 7.
T 93 319 30 98
El Velódromo c/ Muntaner 213.
T 93 430 60 22
La Cova Fumada c/ Baluard, 46.
T 93 221 40 61.
Monvínic c/ Diputació, 249.

T 93 272 61 87. www.monvinic.com
Quimet & Quimet c/ Poeta Cabanyes,
25. T 93 442 31 42.
Tapas 24 c/ Diputació, 269.
T 93 488 09 77. www.comerç24.com
Taktika Berri c/ València, 169.
T 93 453 47 59.
Tickets Av. Paral·lel,164.
T 93 292 42 50. http://es.bcn50.org

Cafés

Café de la Ópera c/ La Rambla, 74.
T 93 317 75 85. www.cafeoperabcn.com
Casa Almirall c/ Joaquín Costa, 33.
T 93 318 9917
Café del Centre c/Girona 69.
T 93 488 11 01
Café Vienés Passeig de Gràcia 132.
T 93 255 30 00.
Demasié Café c/Roger de Llúria, 8
y Princesa, 28. T 678 596 755.
www.demasie.es

Oyster Bars

Fishhh! Centre Comercial Illa Diagonal.
T 93 444 11 39. www.fishhh.net
Gouthier. c/ Mañé i Flaquer, 8.
T 93 205 99 69. www.gouthier.es

Wine Bars

Cata 1.81 c/València, 181.
T 93 323 68 18. www.cata181.com
D.O. c/ Verdi, 36. T 93 218 96 73.

La Vinya del Senyor Plaça de Santa
Maria, 5. T 93 310 33 79.
Monvínic c/ Diputació, 249.
T 93 272 61 87. www.monvinic.com

Cocktails

Boadas c/ Tallers 1. T 93 318 88 26.
Dry Martini c/Aribau, 162-166.
T 93 217 50 72. www.drymartinibcn.com
Gimlet Santaló, 46. T 93 201 53 06.
www.gimletbcn.com
Ideal Cocktail Bar c/ Aribau, 89.
T 93 453 10 28.
www.idealcocktailbar.com

Granges, *orxateries*, **(tiger nut milk
and ice cream parlours)**

Gelateria Pagliotta c/ Jaume I, 15.
T 93 310 53 24. www.pagliotta.com
Granja Viader c/ Xuclà, 4-6.
T 93 318 34 86. www.granjaviader.cat
Granja La Pallaresa c/ Petritxol, 11.
T 93 302 20 36. www.lapallaresa.com
Orchateria La Valenciana
c/ Aribau 16 bis. T 93 317 27 71.
www.lavalenciana.com
Orxateria-Torroneria Sirvent
c/ Parlament 56. 93 441 27 20.
www.turronessirvent.com
Orxateria El Tío Ché c/ Rambla del
Poblenou, 44-46. T 93 309 18 72.
http://eltioche.es

bibliography

Andrews, Colman. *Cuina catalana.* Edicions Martínez Roca. Barcelona. 1990.

Bàguena i Maranges, Núria. *Cuinar i menjar a Barcelona* (1850-1900). CIM Edicions. Barcelona. 2007.

Blasi, Josep Maria. *La cuina d'Ignasi Domènech.* Angle editorial. Barcelona. 2005.

Càlix, Judith; Serret, Cristina. Direcció de continguts: Tana Collados. *"De la terra al rebost: un passeig gastronòmic per la província de Barcelona"* Institut d'Edicions de la Diputació de Barcelona. Barcelona. 2003.

Collados, Tana y Olivella, Àgata. *Al vostre gust.* Cossetània Edicions. Valls. 2009.

Casas, Carmen. *Barcelona a la carta.* Editorial Laia. Barcelona. 1981.

Domènech, Joan de Déu. *Xocolata cada dia. A taula amb el baró do Maldà.* Edicions La Magrana. Barcelona. 2004.

Eymoric, Clovis. *El hostal, la fonda, la taberna y el café en la vida barcelonesa.* Editorial Milà. Barcelona. 1945

Fàbrega, Jaume. *El gust d'un poble.* Edicions Cossetània. Valls (Tarragona). 2002.

Gasull, Carme. *Cataluña en ol paladar.* Ed. Austral Media. Barcelona. 2004.

Luján, Néstor. *El ritual del aperitivo: avisillos, llamativos y tapas.* Ediciones Folio. Barcelona. 1995.

Luján, Néstor. *Vint segles de cuina a Barcelona.* Ediciones Folio. Barcelona 1973.

Lladonosa i Giró, Josep. *El gran llibre de la cuina catalana.* Edicions Península. Barcelona. 1992.

Martí Escayol, Maria Antònia. *El plaer do la xocolata: la història i cultura de la xocolata a Catalunya.* Edicions Cossetània. Valls (Tarragona). 2004.

Mas, Jorge. *Barcelona Gourmand.* Viena Edicions. Barcelona. 2008.

Permanyer, Lluís. *L'esplendor de la Barcelona burgesa.* Angle editorial. Barcelona. 2010.

Pla, Josep. *El que hem menjat.* Ediciones Destino. Barcelona. 1981.

Rondissoni, José. *Culinaria.* Antonio Bosch, editor. Sexta edición. Barcelona. 1945.

Vázquez Montalbán, Manuel. *La cocina catalana.* Ediciones Península. Barcelona. 1979.

Villar, Paco. *La ciutat dels cafés.* Barcelona 1750-1880. Edicions La Campana i Ajuntament de Barcelona. Barcelona. 2008.

VV.AA. *Del rebost a la taula.* Cuina i menjar a la Barcelona gòtica. Museu d'Història de la Ciutat de Barcelona. Ed. Electa. Barcelona. 1994.

glossary

Beco: name by which some of the first restaurants in Barcelona were known, run by Italian chefs. In his book *Veinte siglos de cocina en Barcelona*, Néstor Luján explains that a Sardinian restaurateur, arriving in the city in 1788, opened the "Beco del Racó" in 1815, where he served stewed hare, potato stew, *escudella* broth, meatball soup, fricassee...

Carn d'olla: meats and sausages that are used to prepare the *escudella* broth. First the soup is served, with galetti or another pasta and then the *carn d'olla*. Generally, it includes chicken, pig's ear, pig's snout and trotters, lamb or beef hock, blood sausage... Also not to be missed is the *pilota*, a large meatball made with minced beef and pork, and seasoned with garlic and parsley.

Carquinyolis: typical sweet cakes, made with flour, sugar, eggs and almonds or hazelnuts. The mass, in the form of a flat trunk, is cut into slices which are then baked.

Coca: flat cake typical all over the Mediterranean with multiple sweet and savoury variants.

Cul de café: the "dregs" of the coffee, the amusing name given to the person in charge of livening up the chats at the café.

Escalfeta: portable brazier, generally made of tin or brass, which was used to heat the first cafés in the city.

Escudella: bowl in which soups and stews were served in the Middle Ages. The word ended up being associated with the name of one of the most popular dishes of Catalan cuisine.

Foams: light mousses made from gelatinised purées, creams or juices with the help of a siphon loaded with N2O. In 1994 Ferran Adrià created a mythical dish: the texture stew. He incorporated new vanguard concepts, such as "deconstruction" and the foams, and represents a turning point in the history of creative cuisine.

Fonda: first establishments in which they served meals. A charming and much loved chronicler from Barcelona, Sempronio (Andreu Avel·lí Artís), explained that the word comes from the Arab *alfondek*, a type of warehouse that traders optimise also using it to eat and sleep in.

Fricassee: beef stew with dried mushrooms, previously rehydrated.

Garum: sauce from the Roman period which was made with the juices of fermented blue fish tripe. It was exported by sea trading routes, bottled in amphorae, to other colonies of the empire.

Granges: cafeterias that, in their origin, were specialised in selling dairy products.

Llardons: pork scratchings. They are used to prepare the *coca de llardons*, typical of Fat Thursday and the days of Carnival.

Llauna: tin. It gives its name to the recipes that, in their origin, were prepared directly on a tin oven plate. Very popular are cod and snails *a la llauna*.

Mató: cottage cheese.

Mona: typical Easter cake. Originally, tradition required that on Easter Monday the godparents gave their godchildren a cake decorated with eggs. At the end of the 19th century, some confectioners from Mallorca living in Barcelona made it popular to decorate the cakes with chocolate figures, some of which represented a monkey, *mona*.

Mostassaf or mostaçaf: public post of the municipal administration, instituted in the 14th century. His function was to safeguard the economic interests of consumers, equity in trade and vigilance of abusive practices in the markets.

Neules: sweets or wafers in a cylindrical form, typical at Christmas time.

glossary

Nyora: dry spice pepper. Once soaked to rehydrate it, its pulp is used to prepare the *calçot*, *xató* or *romescu* sauces.

Panellets: sweets made with marzipan, absolutely essential, along with sweet potatoes and chestnuts, to celebrate All Saints Day.

Rovellons: Paulet. In principle, *rovellons* are only *Lactarius sanguifluus*, of a wine red colour with purple latex. Generically, and mistakenly, also called *rovellons* are *pinetells*, saffron milk caps (*Lactarius deliciosus*), more orangey in colour. There are other popular names for these mushrooms, such as *esclatasangs* or *vinaders*.

Samfaina: ratatouille, a preparation of stewed vegetables, generally aubergines, peppers and onion.

Spherification: mixing liquids, infusions or creams with alginates, and submerging drops of liquid in a bath of calcium chloride, small balls are obtained. This is how recipes such as caviar of melon or false olives are created. It is a technique developed in Taller de el Bulli in 2003.

Suís: hot chocolate that is usually served covered with whipped cream. It is one of the most typical specialties of the city *granges*.

Teca: popularly, meal.

Tortell: ring-shaped cake.

Xató: escarole salad with anchovies, cod, tuna and olives, typical of the area of El Garraf and El Penedès. It is also the name of the sauce made with toasted almonds and hazelnuts, breadcrumbs soaked in vinegar, olive oil, garlic and pulp of ñora pepper.

index of recipes

kidney beans with streaky bacon
and *botifarra* sausage ... 138

cuban rice ... 140

barcelona rice ... 143

cod rice ... 144

parellada rice ... 146

cod fritters ... 149

cannelloni *a la barcelonesa* ... 150

empedrat salted cod with white beans ... 152

russian salad ... 154

escalivada baked vegetables ... 156

escudella barrejada mixed broth ... 158

escudella i carn d'olla
broth with stewed meat ... 160

spinach with raisins and pine nuts ... 162

esqueixada cod salad ... 164

casseroled noodles ... 167

chick peas with cod and spinach ... 168

sautéed peas and broad beans ... 170

broad beans *a la catalana* ... 173

montcorrat tomatoes with anchovies ... 174

fat thursday omelette ... 176

xató almond and hazelnut sauce ... 179

hake meatballs ... 182

cod *a la llauna* in the pan ... 184

cod *a la manresana* ... 187

cod with honey ... 188

calamari filled with chocolate sauce ... 190

gaudí red mullets of ferran adrià ... 193

baby cuttlefish a la barcelonesa ... 194

sarsuela ... 196

cap i pota with *samfaina*
head and leg of beef with ratatouille ... 199

rabbit with chocolate ... 200

fricandó fricassee ... 202

pork loin kidney beans ... 205

pigs trotters filled with wild
mushrooms and prawns ... 206

roast chicken with *samfaina* ratatouille ... 208

beef with wild mushrooms ... 211

swiss roll ... 214

lent fritters ... 216

pork scratching flat cake ... 219

saint john's flat cake ... 220

catalan custard ... 222

foams of sitges ... 225

panellets catalan almond
cookies with pine nuts ... 226

sweet potato pudding ... 228

cottage cheese with honey ... 231

barcelona_cuisine

acknowledgements

Aurora Bofarull (Los Caracoles), Montserrat Agut
(Can Culleretes), Els 4 Gats, Marc Cuspinera (El Bulli), Rafael
Penya (Restaurante Gresca), Ramon Solé i Pere Pina (Casa
Almirall), Flavia Silva, Carles Abellán (Tapas 24), Bar Cañete,
Cafè del Centre, Christian Escribà, Jordi Butrón (Espai Sucre),
Sr. Carulla, Colmado Quílez, Chocolatería Fargas, Pastisseria
Brunells, Granja La Pallaresa, Oriol Balaguer, Frutas Soley
i comerciants del Mercat de la Boqueria, Jordi González
(Mercabarna), Confraria de Pescadors de Barcelona, La Cova
Fumada, Santi (Horticultura Noé), Bodegas Alta Alella, Xarel·lo,
Marc (Hortetdelbaix), Miquel Mestres i Maria Palós, Sonia
Callao (Parc Agrari del Baix Llobregat), Xavier Giménez, Manuel
(Granja Torres), Família Llopart (Caves Llopart), Can Feixes,
Quimet & Quimet, Cafés El Magnífico, Jamonísimo, La Casa
del Bacalao, Dry Martini, Casa Gispert, Fleca Fortino,
Monvínic, Caelum, Joan Múrria (Queviures Múrria), Museu
de la Xocolata, Granja Viader, Orchateria Sirvent, Quim i Eva
Vila (Vilaviniteca), El Xampanyet, Biblioteca de Catalunya,
Arxiu Històric de la Ciutat de Barcelona, Arxiu Fotogràfic de
Barcelona, Ateneu Barcelonès. Fundació Josep Pla.